D1239955

Road Atlas of

Rockingham County

New Hampshire

DISCLAIMER

Information shown on these maps is compiled from multiple sources and may not be complete or accurate. This product is for entertainment purposes only and is not a land survey. The author cannot be held responsible for misuse or misinterpretation of any information and offers no warranty, guarantees, or representations of any kind in connection to its accuracy or completeness. This product is not intended as medical, legal, business, financial, or safety advice. The author accepts no liability for any loss, damage, injury, or inconvenience caused as a result of reliance on this product.

Data Sources:

U.S. Census Bureau

U.S. Fish & Wildlife Service

U.S. Geological Survey

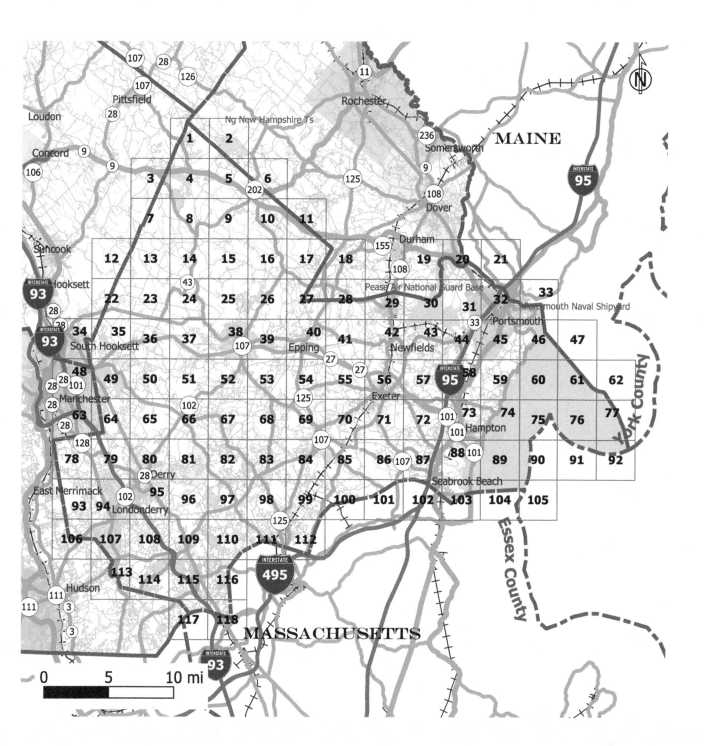

LEGEND

County Boundary		Cliff	
Township Boundary		Dam/Levee	
Municipal Boundary		Falls	
Water		Harbor	
Military Installation		Heliport	
Native American Area		Hospital	
Park		Mine	
Interstate Highway		Park	
US Route		Post Office	
State Route		School	
Local Road		Spring	
Railway		Summit	
Airport		Tower	
Cemetery		Well	
Church			

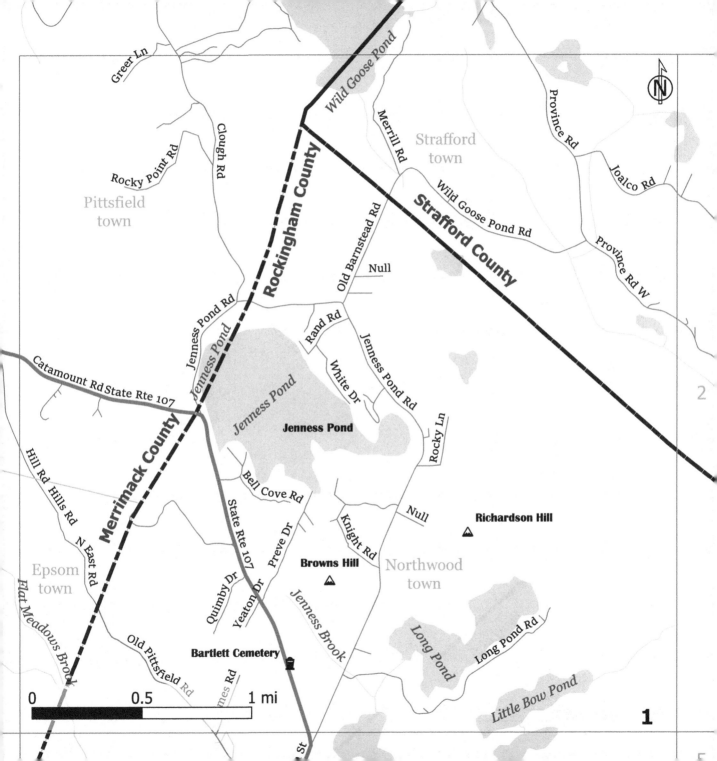

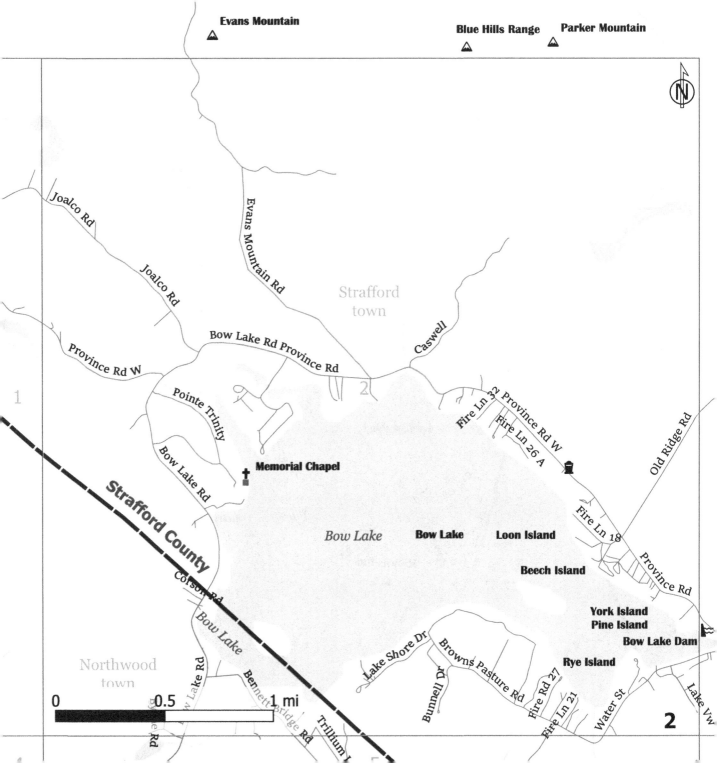

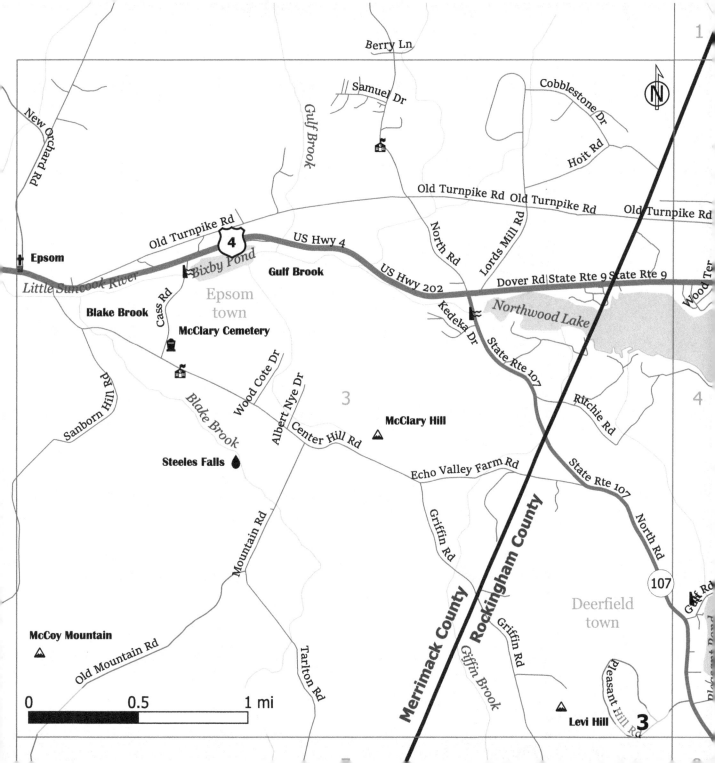

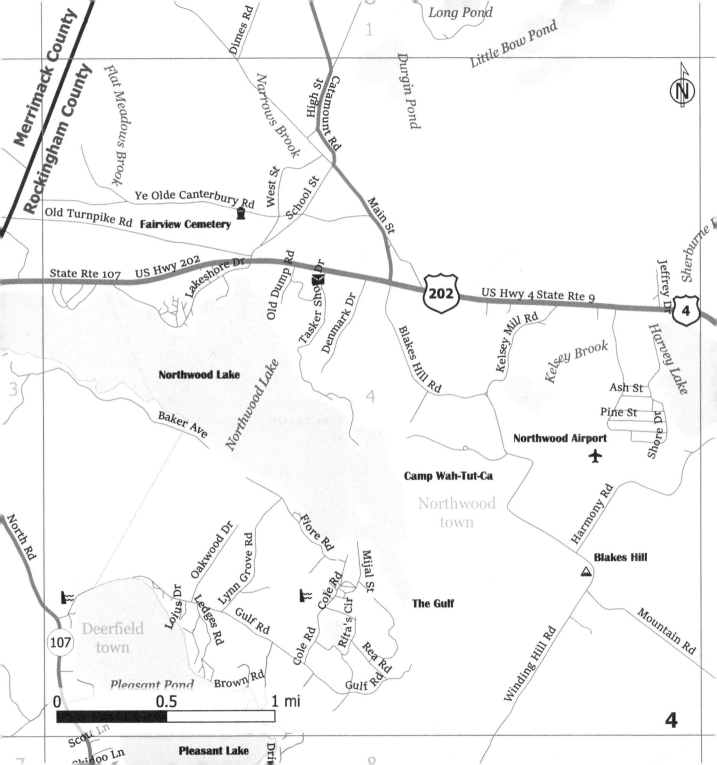

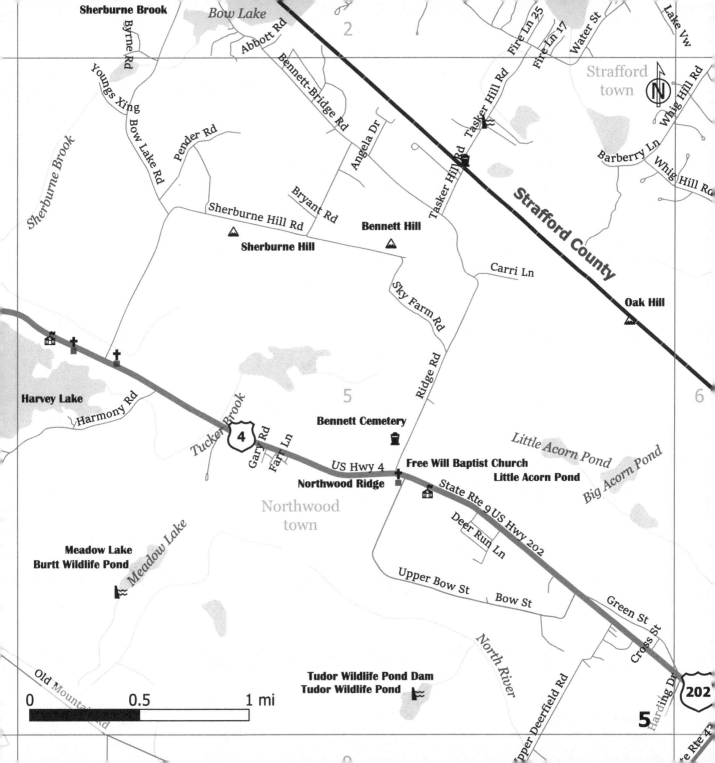

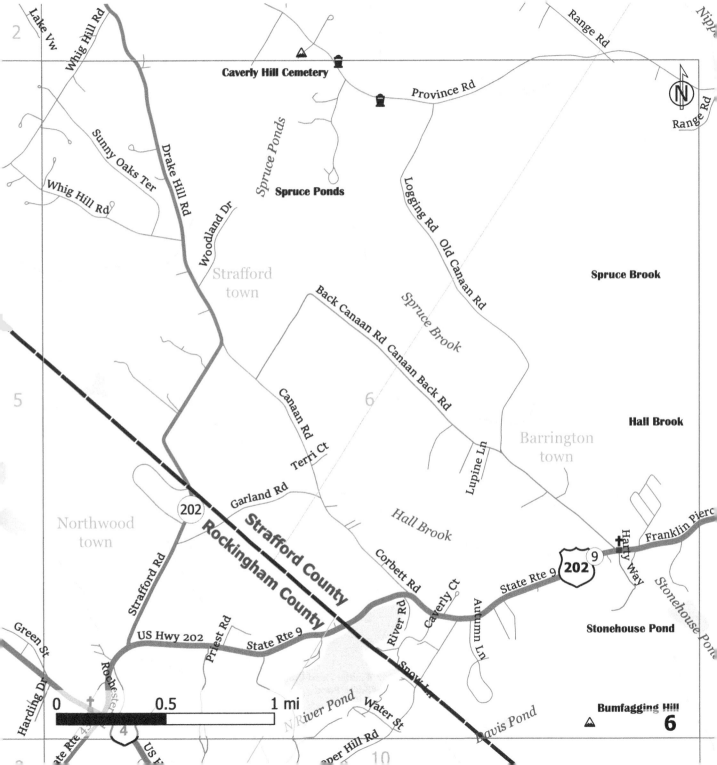

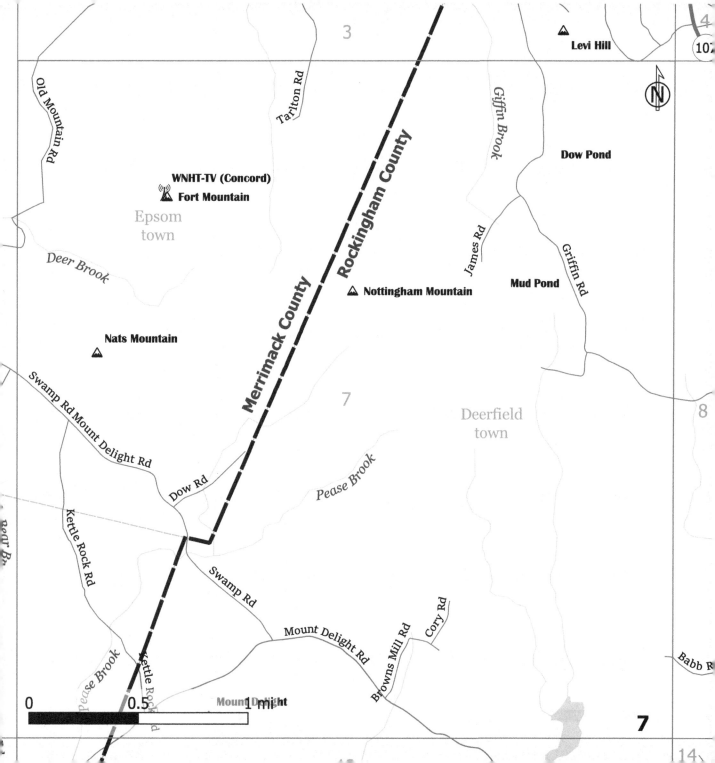

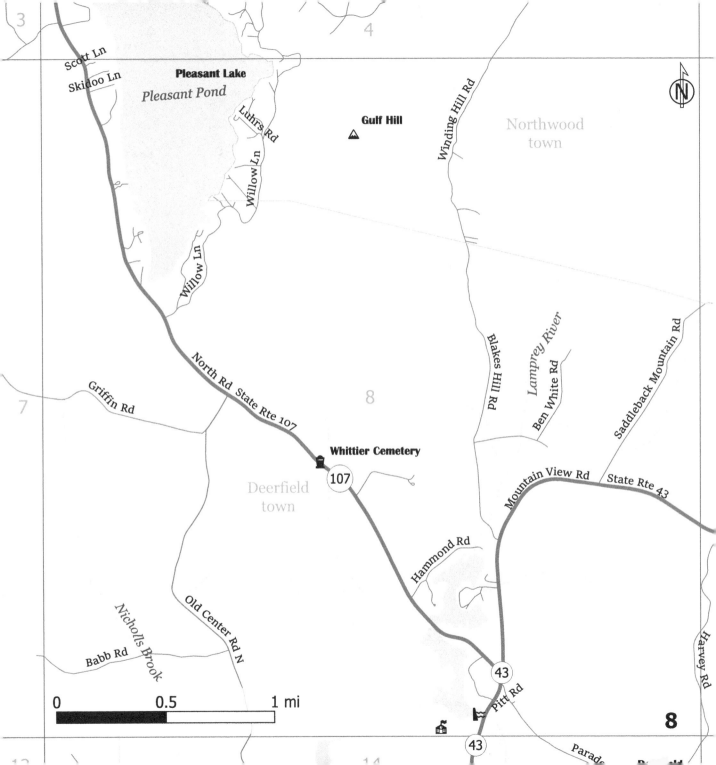

4

Scott Ln

Skidoo Ln

Pleasant Lake

Pleasant Pond

Luhrs Rd

Gulf Hill

Winding Hill Rd

Northwood town

Willow Ln

Willow Ln

North Rd State Rte 107

Griffin Rd

8

Blakes Hill Rd

Lamprey River

Ben White Rd

Saddleback Mountain Rd

Whittier Cemetery

107

Deerfield town

Mountain View Rd   State Rte 43

Hammond Rd

Nicholls Brook

Old Center Rd N

Babb Rd

Harvey Rd

43

Pitt Rd

0   0.5   1 mi

8

43

Parade

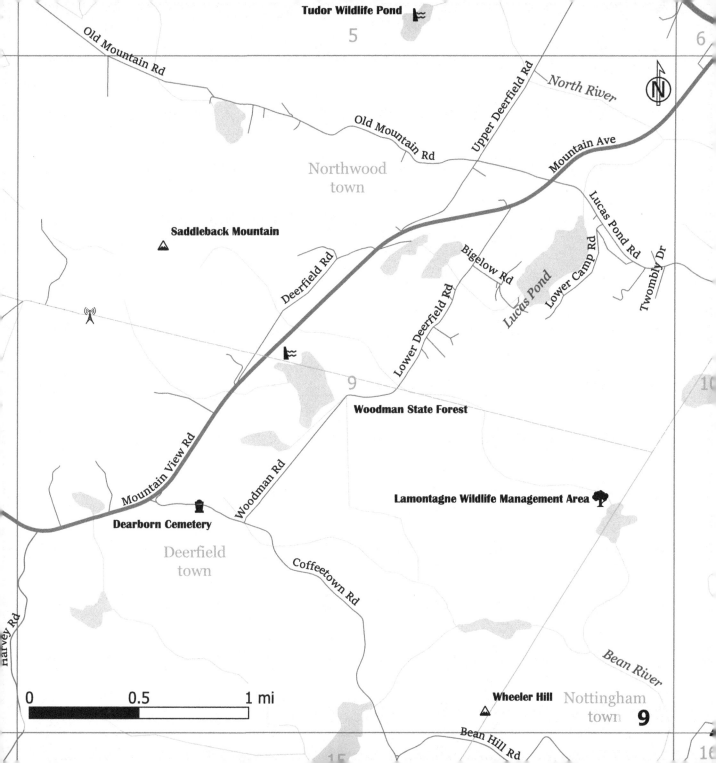

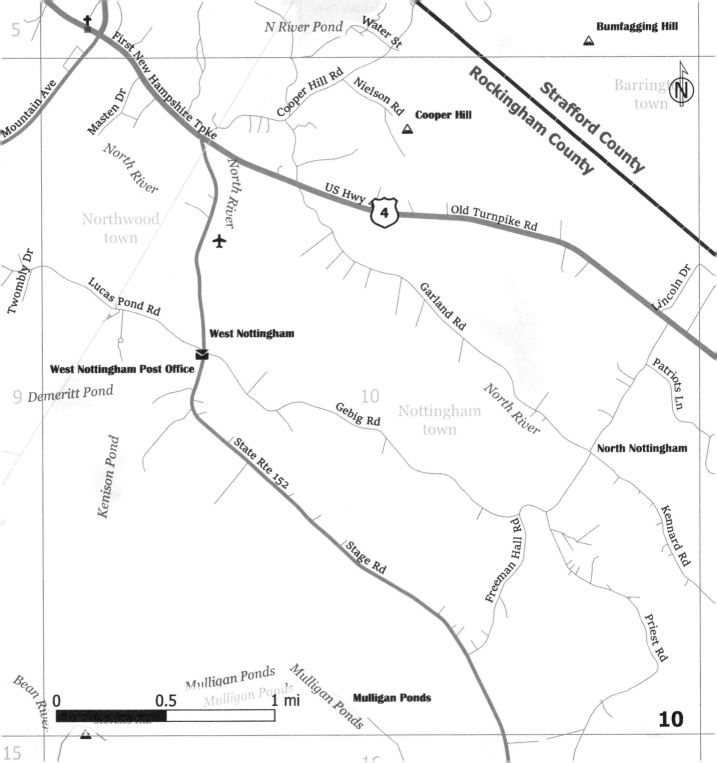

5

N River Pond

Water St

Bumfagging Hill

Mountain Ave

First New Hampshire Tpke

Masten Dr

North River

Cooper Hill Rd

Nielson Rd

Cooper Hill

Rockingham County

Strafford County

Barrington town

N

North River

Northwood town

US Hwy 4

4

Old Turnpike Rd

Twombly Dr

Lucas Pond Rd

Garland Rd

Lincoln Dr

West Nottingham

West Nottingham Post Office

9 Demeritt Pond

North River

Nottingham town

10

Gebig Rd

Patriots Ln

North Nottingham

Kenison Pond

State Rte 152

Freeman Hall Rd

Kennard Rd

Stage Rd

Priest Rd

Bean River

Mulligan Ponds

Mulligan Ponds

Mulligan Ponds

Mulligan Ponds

Stevens Hill

0   0.5   1 mi

10

15

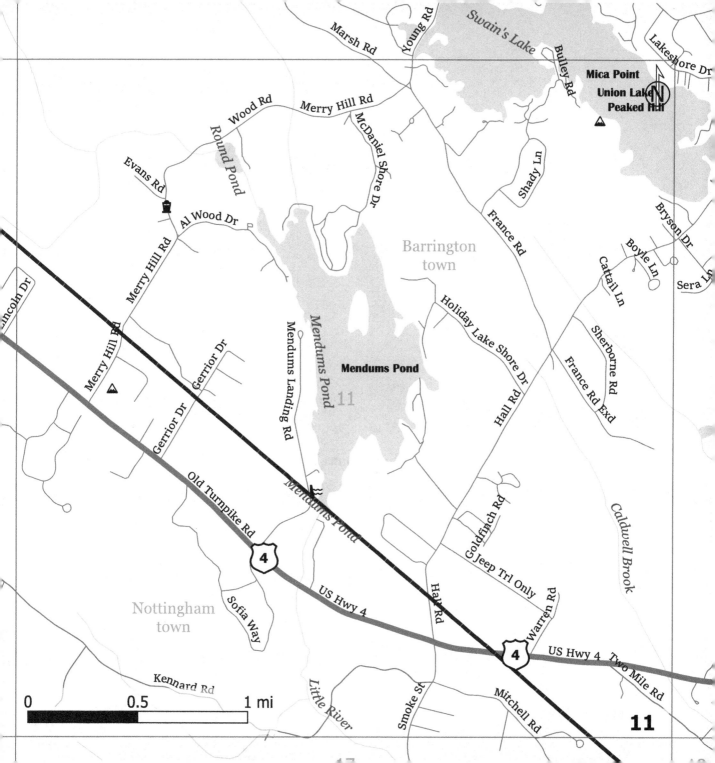

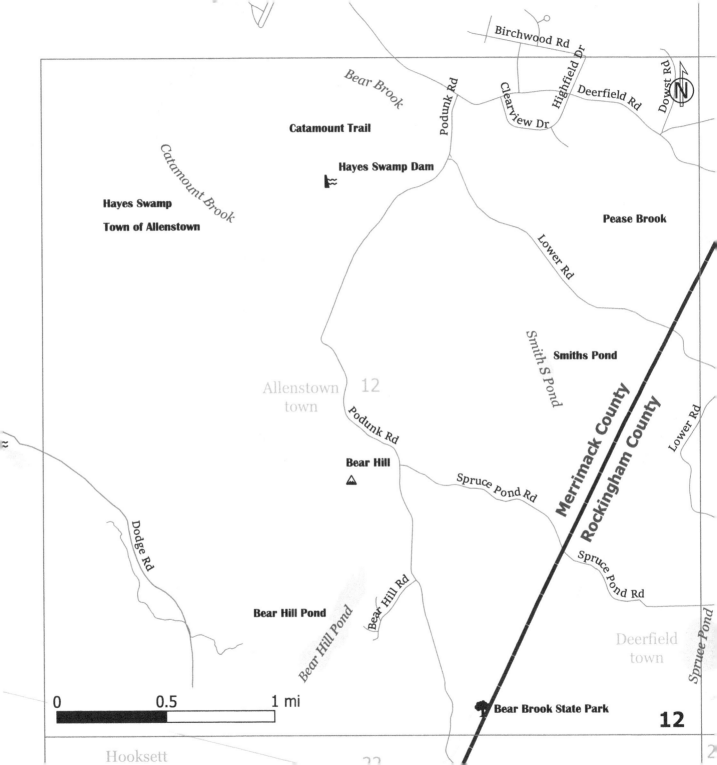

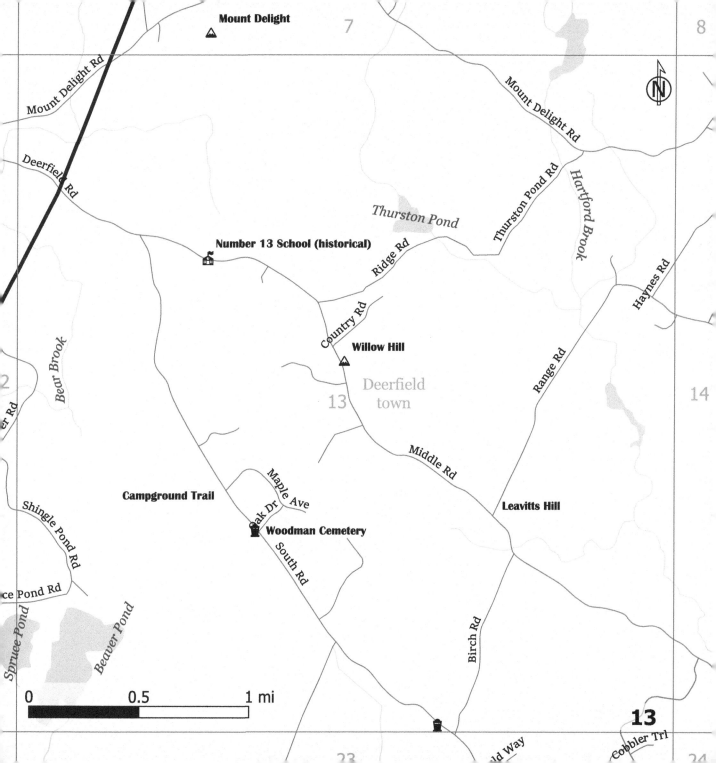

Mount Delight

7

8

Mount Delight Rd

Mount Delight Rd

Deerfield Rd

Hartford Brook

Thurston Pond

Thurston Pond Rd

Number 13 School (historical)

Ridge Rd

Haynes Rd

Country Rd

Willow Hill

Deerfield town

13

Bear Brook

Range Rd

2

14

Middle Rd

Campground Trail

Maple Ave

Leavitts Hill

Shingle Pond Rd

Oak Dr

Woodman Cemetery

ce Pond Rd

South Rd

Spruce Pond

Beaver Pond

Birch Rd

0   0.5   1 mi

13

23

ld Way

Cobbler Trl

24

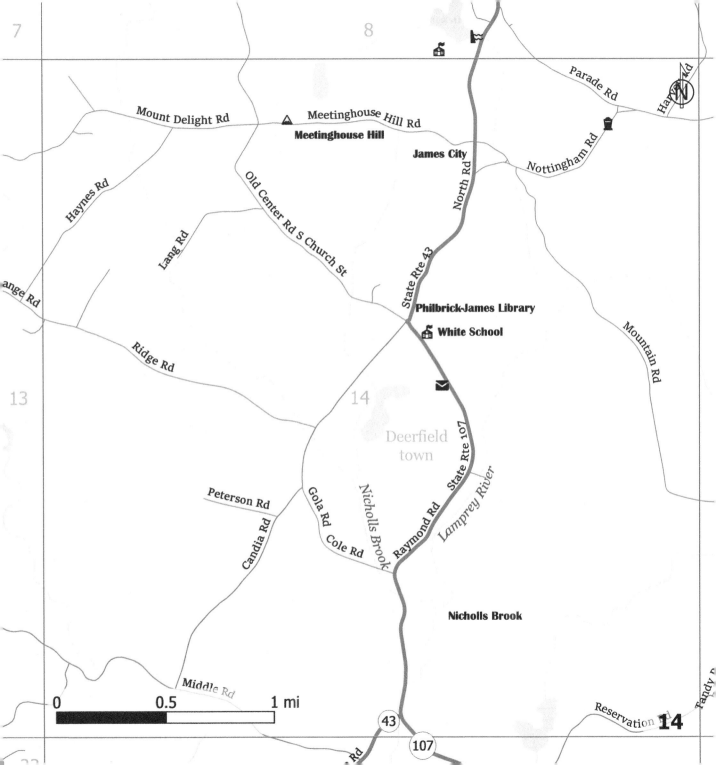

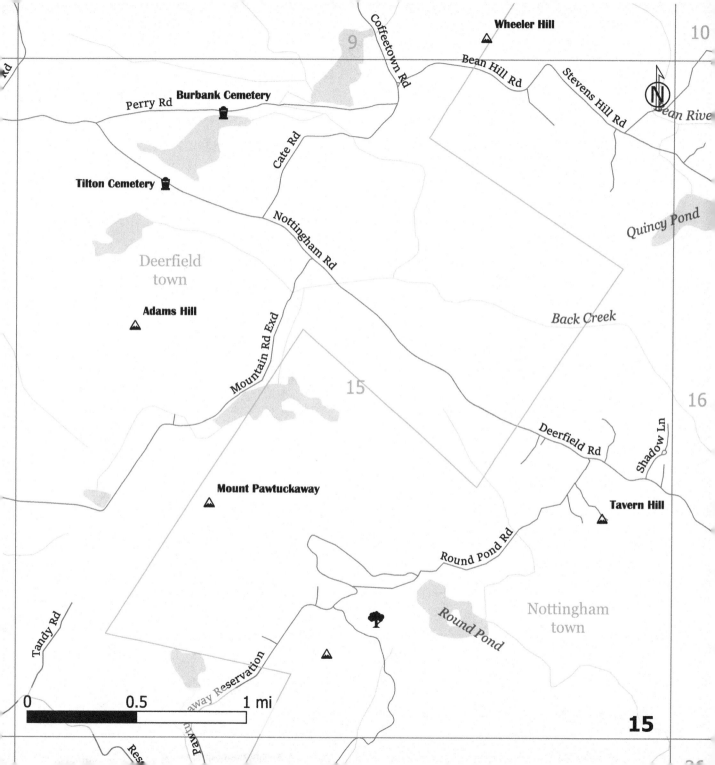

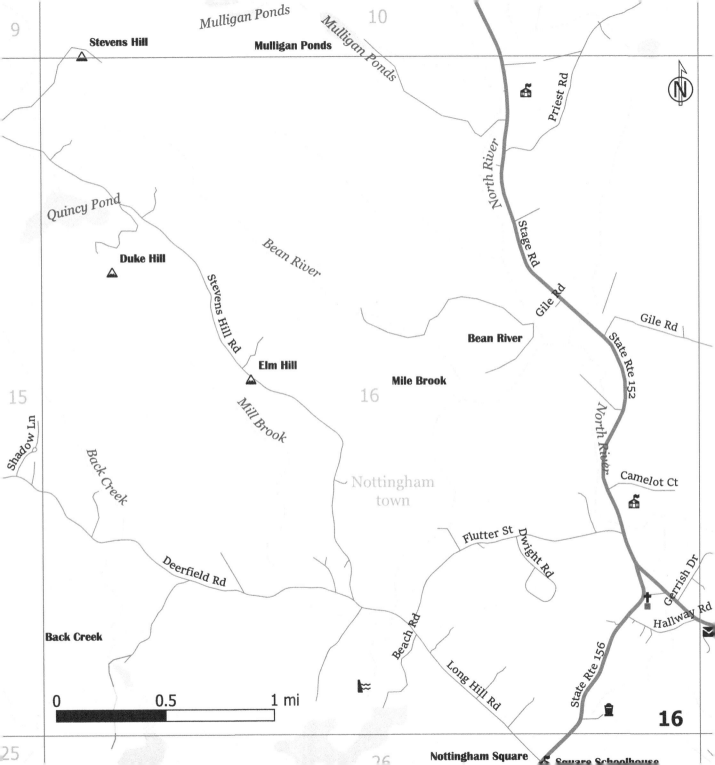

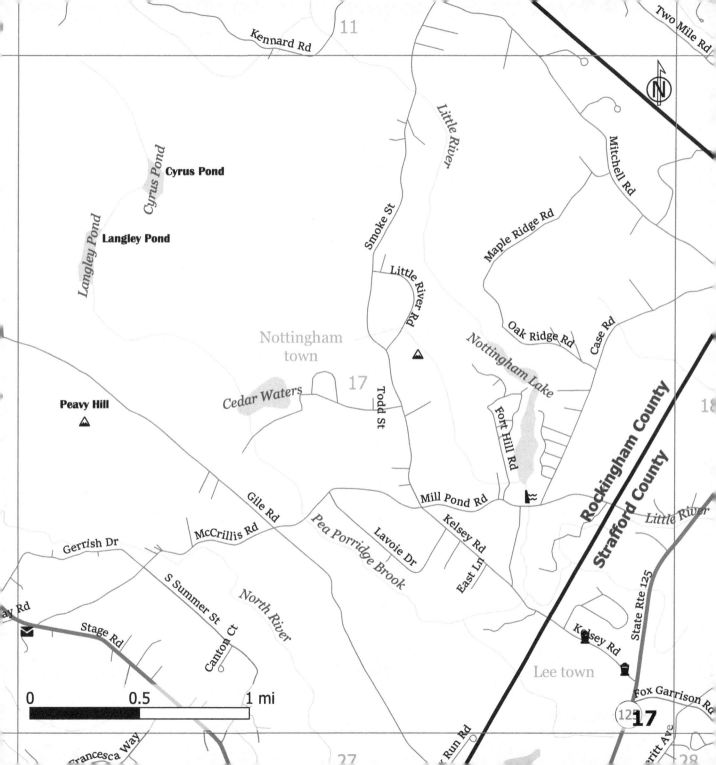

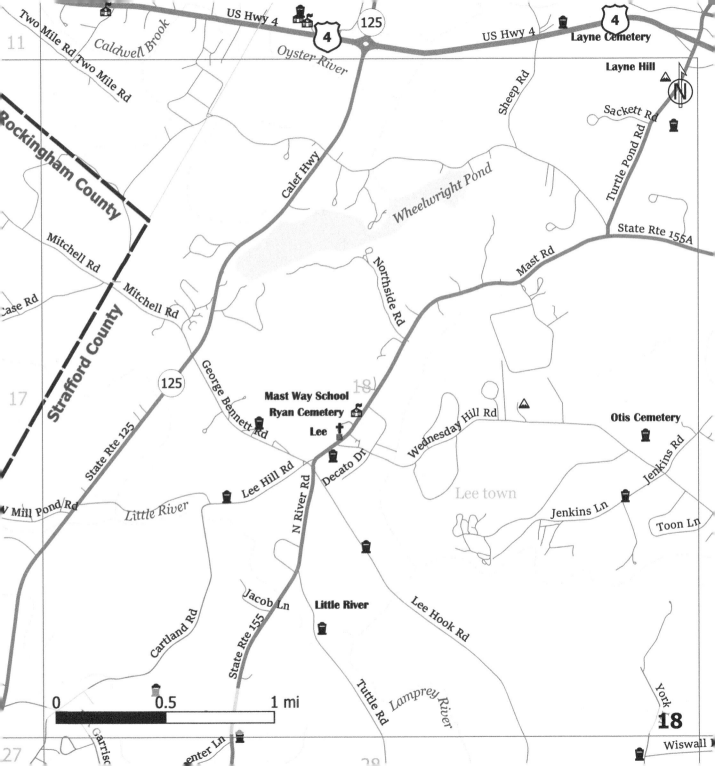

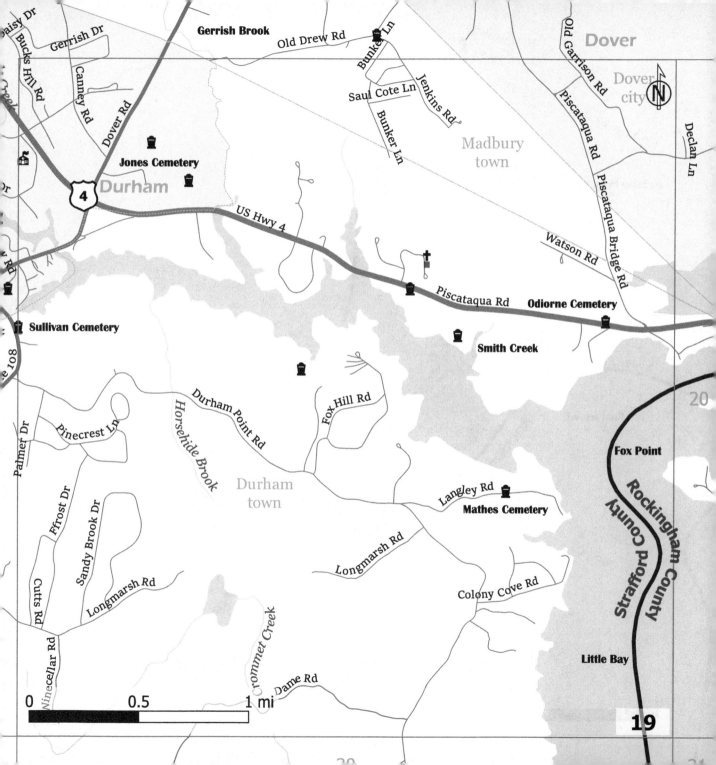

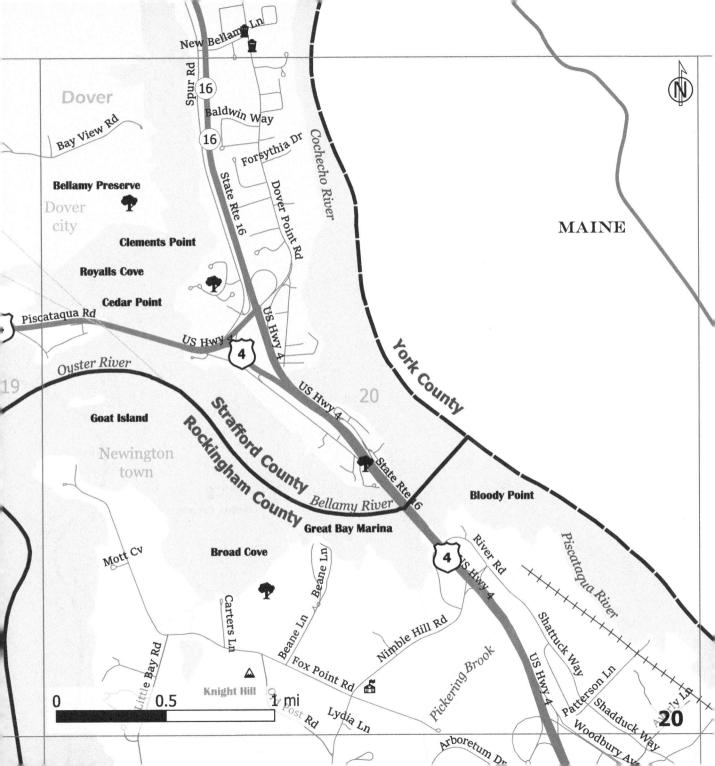

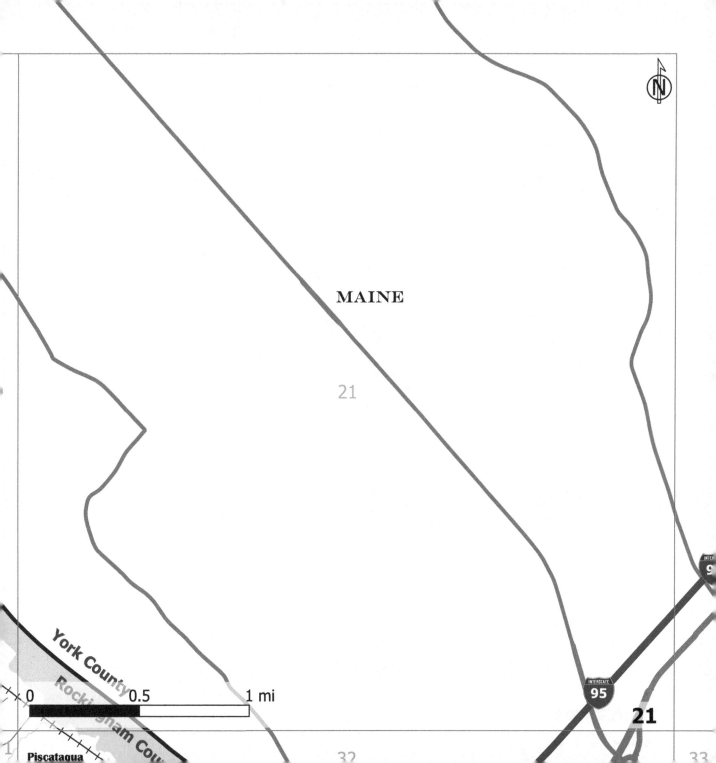

MAINE

21

York County

Rockingham Cou

Piscataqua

0   0.5   1 mi

21

95

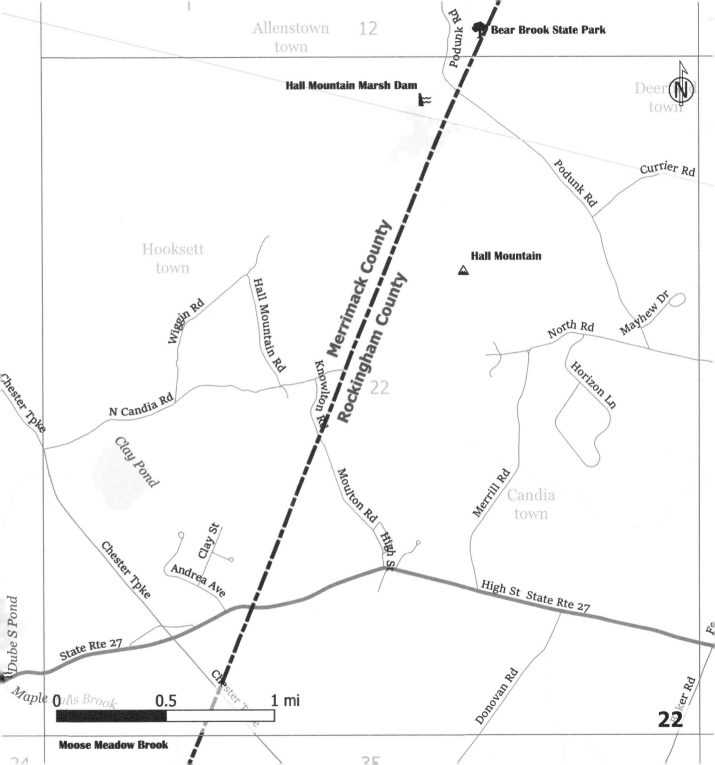

Allenstown
town
12

Bear Brook State Park

Hall Mountain Marsh Dam

Deerfield
town

Currier Rd

Podunk Rd

Podunk Rd

Hooksett
town

Merrimack County

Rockingham County

22

Hall Mountain

Mayhew Dr

North Rd

Horizon Ln

Wiggin Rd

Hall Mountain Rd

Chester Tpke

N Candia Rd

Knowlton Rd

Clay Pond

Merrill Rd

Candia
town

Clay St

Moulton Rd

High St

Chester Tpke

Andrea Ave

Dube S Pond

High St State Rte 27

State Rte 27

Donovan Rd

Maple

Bulls Brook

Chester Tpke

0   0.5   1 mi

22

Moose Meadow Brook

34

35

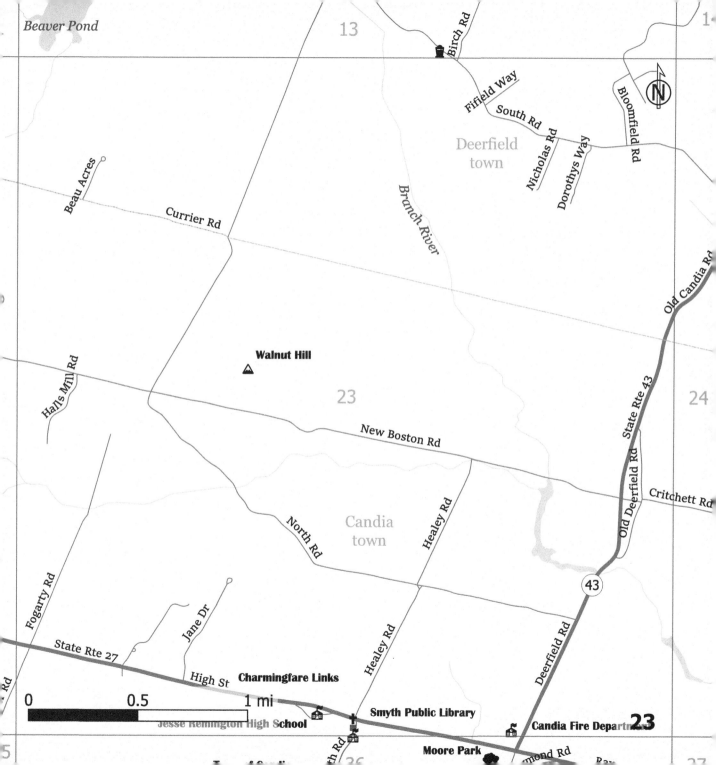

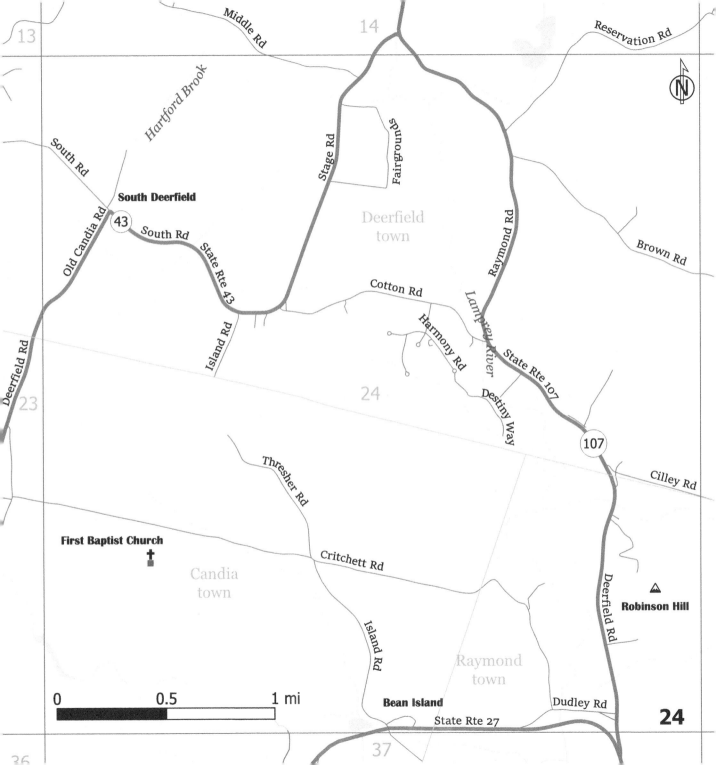

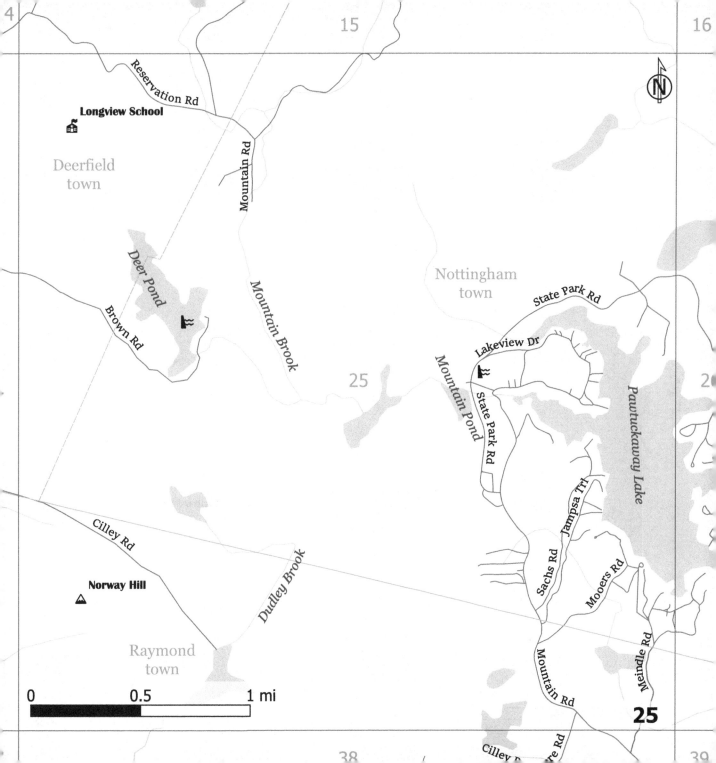

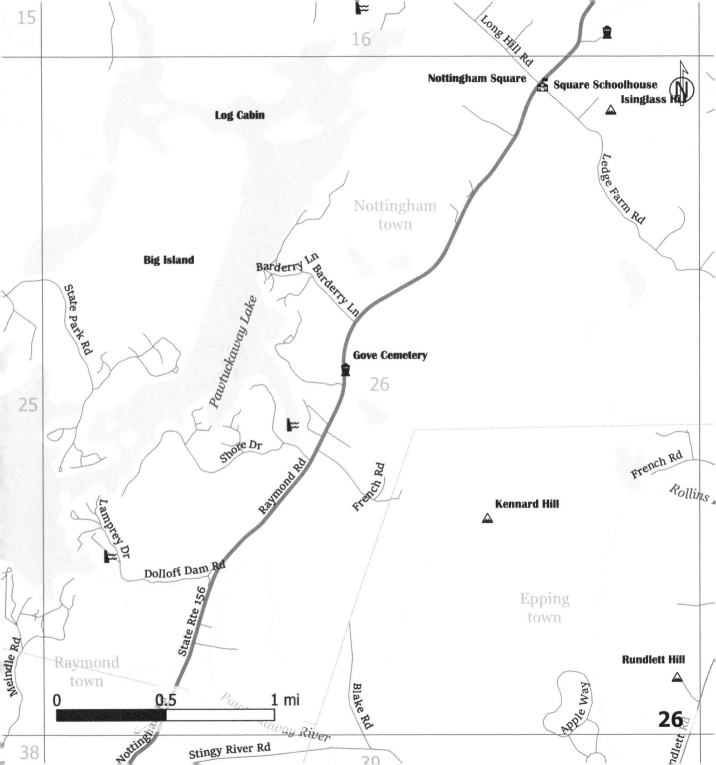

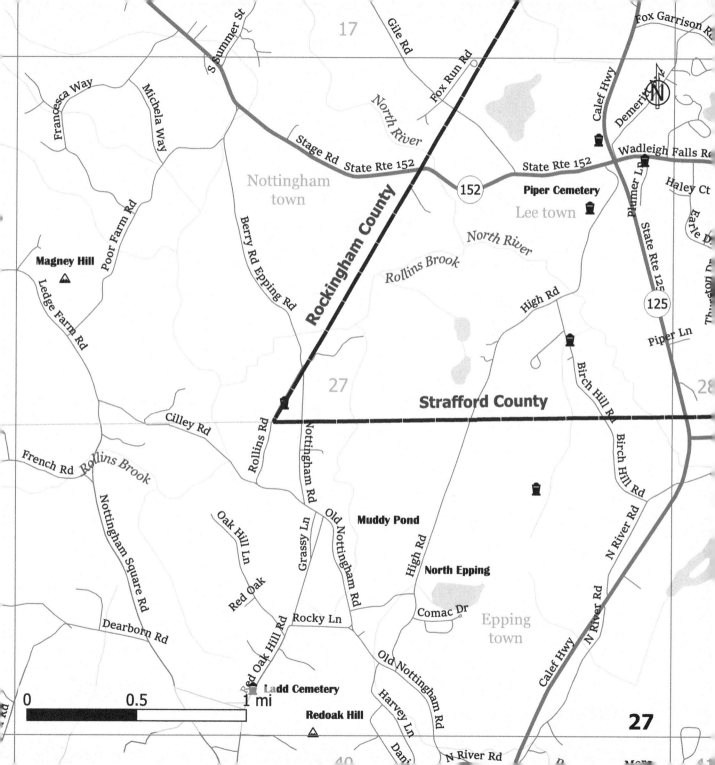

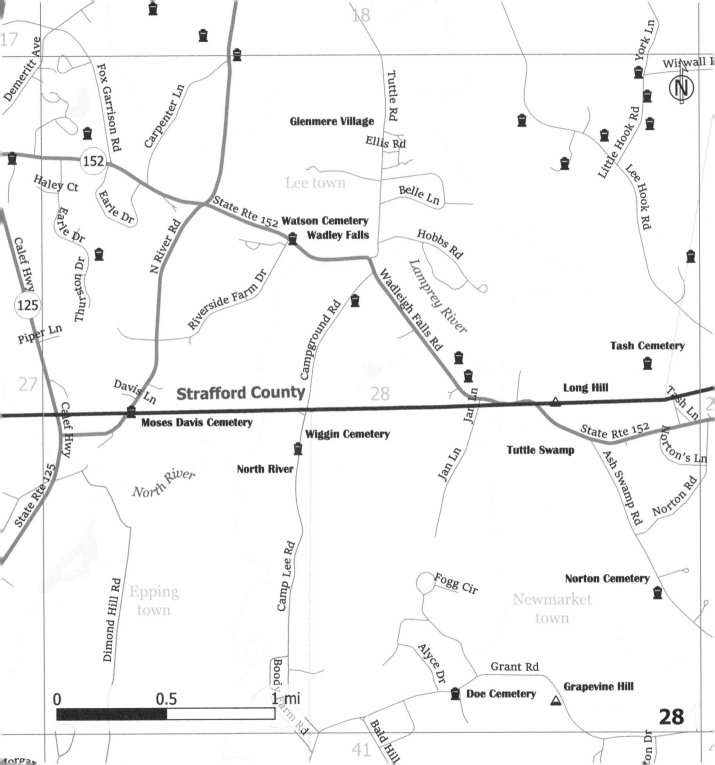

17

18

Demeritt Ave

Fox Garrison Rd

Carpenter Ln

Glenmere Village

Tuttle Rd

Ellis Rd

Lee town

152

Haley Ct

Earle Dr

Earle Dr

Thurston Dr

N River Rd

State Rte 152

Belle Ln

Hobbs Rd

Wiswall

York Ln

Little Hook Rd

Lee Hook Rd

N

Watson Cemetery
Wadley Falls

Calef Hwy

125

Piper Ln

Riverside Farm Dr

Campground Rd

Wadleigh Falls Rd

Lamprey River

Tash Cemetery

Davis Ln

Strafford County

28

Jan Ln

Long Hill

Tash Ln

2

Calef Hwy

Moses Davis Cemetery

State Rte 152

Norton's Ln

Wiggin Cemetery

Tuttle Swamp

Ash Swamp Rd

Norton Rd

State Rte 125

North River

North River

Jan Ln

Norton Cemetery

Epping
town

Dimond Hill Rd

Camp Lee Rd

Fogg Cir

Newmarket
town

Alyce Dr

Grant Rd

Grapevine Hill

Doe Cemetery

Boody Farm Rd

Bald Hill

27

0   0.5   1 mi

41

28

Morga

on Dr

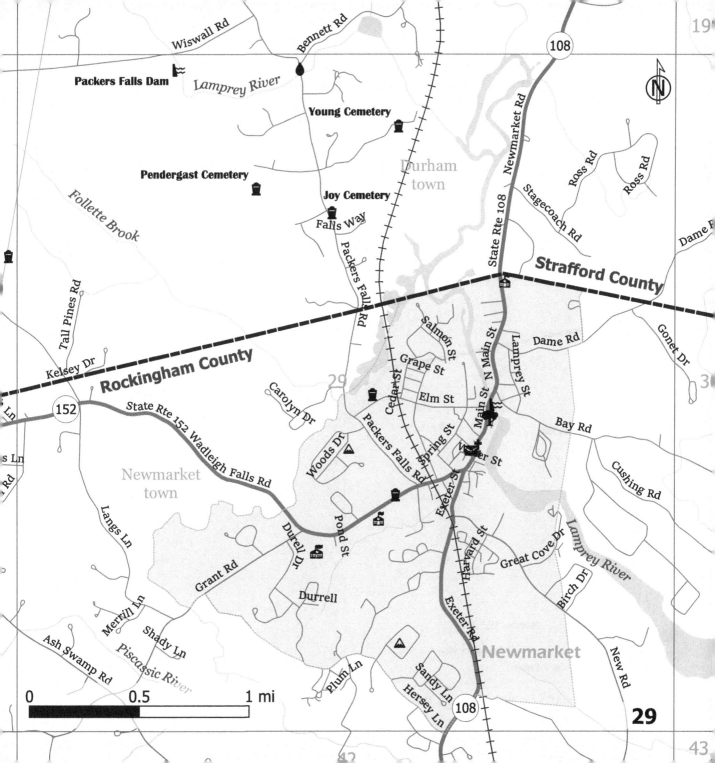

Wiswall Rd

Bennett Rd

108

Packers Falls Dam

Lamprey River

Newmarket Rd

Young Cemetery

Ross Rd

Ross Rd

Durham town

Pendergast Cemetery

State Rte 108

Stagecoach Rd

Follette Brook

Joy Cemetery

Falls Way

Packers Falls Rd

Dame R

Strafford County

Salmon St

Dame Rd

Gonet Dr

Kelsey Dr

Rockingham County

Grape St

N Main St

Tall Pines Rd

29

Cedar St

Elm St

Lamprey St

Ln

Carolyn Dr

Bay Rd

152

State Rte 152 Wadleigh Falls Rd

Packers Falls Rd

Spring St

Main St

Water St

Cushing Rd

Woods Dr

Rd

Newmarket town

Langs Ln

Exeter St

Great Cove Dr

Lamprey River

Grant Rd

Durell Dr

Pond St

Harvard St

Birch Dr

Merrill Ln

Durrell

Exeter Rd

Newmarket

New Rd

Ash Swamp Rd

Shady Ln

Piscassic River

Plum Ln

Sandy Ln

108

29

Hersey Ln

0   0.5   1 mi

43

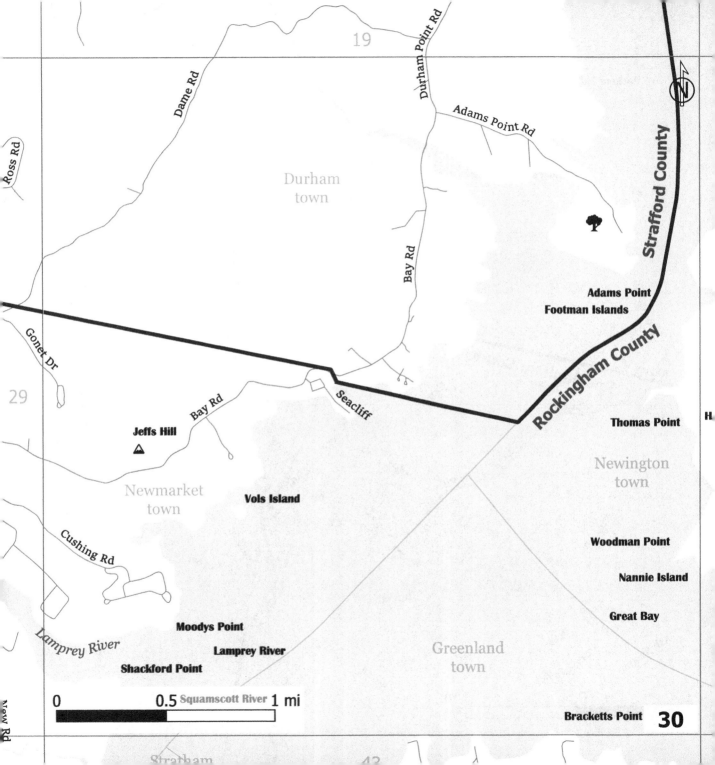

Dame Rd

Durham Point Rd

Adams Point Rd

Ross Rd

Durham
town

Bay Rd

Strafford County

Adams Point

Footman Islands

Gonet Dr

Rockingham County

Seacliff

Thomas Point

Bay Rd

Jeffs Hill

Newington
town

Newmarket
town

Vols Island

Cushing Rd

Woodman Point

Nannie Island

Great Bay

Lamprey River

Moodys Point

Lamprey River

Greenland
town

Shackford Point

New Rd

0   0.5 Squamscott River 1 mi

Bracketts Point **30**

Stratham   42

H

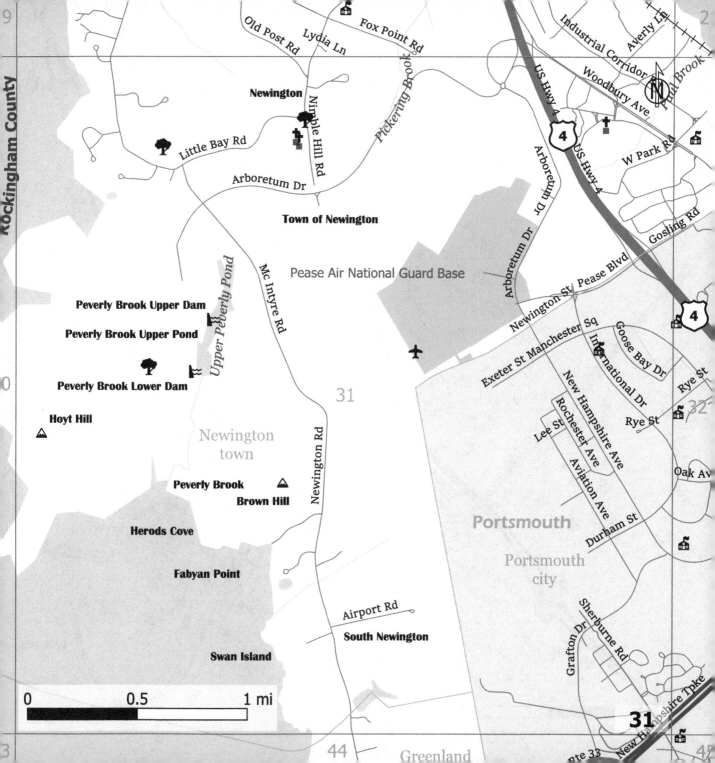

9

ROCKINGHAM County

Old Post Rd
Lydia Ln
Fox Point Rd
Industrial Corridor
Averly Ln
Woodbury Ave
Trut Brook
N

Newington

Nirnble Hill Rd
Pickering Brook
US Hwy 4
4
US Hwy 4
W Park Rd

Little Bay Rd

Arboretum Dr

Arboretum Dr

Gosling Rd

Town of Newington

Pease Air National Guard Base

Arboretum Dr

4

Newington St Pease Blvd

Upper Peverly Pond

Mc Intyre Rd

Peverly Brook Upper Dam

Peverly Brook Upper Pond

Exeter St Manchester Sq
International Dr
Goose Bay Dr
Rye St

Peverly Brook Lower Dam

New Hampshire Ave
Rye St
32

Hoyt Hill

31

Lee St
Rochester Ave
Oak Av

Newington town

Newington Rd

Aviation Ave

Peverly Brook

Brown Hill

Portsmouth

Herods Cove

Durham St

Portsmouth city

Fabyan Point

Grafton Dr
Sherburne Rd

Airport Rd

South Newington

Swan Island

0   0.5   1 mi

31

44   Greenland   Rte 33   New Hampshire Tpke   4

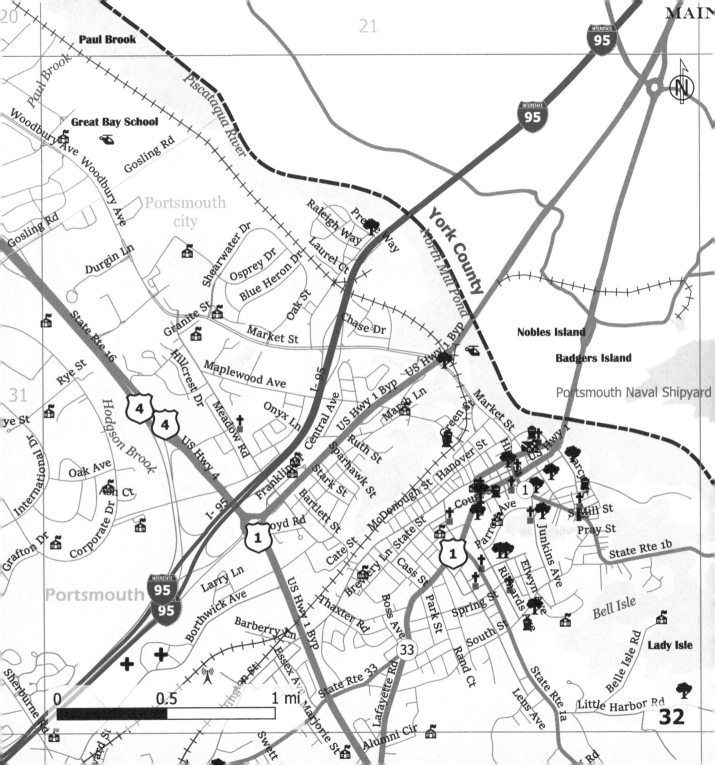

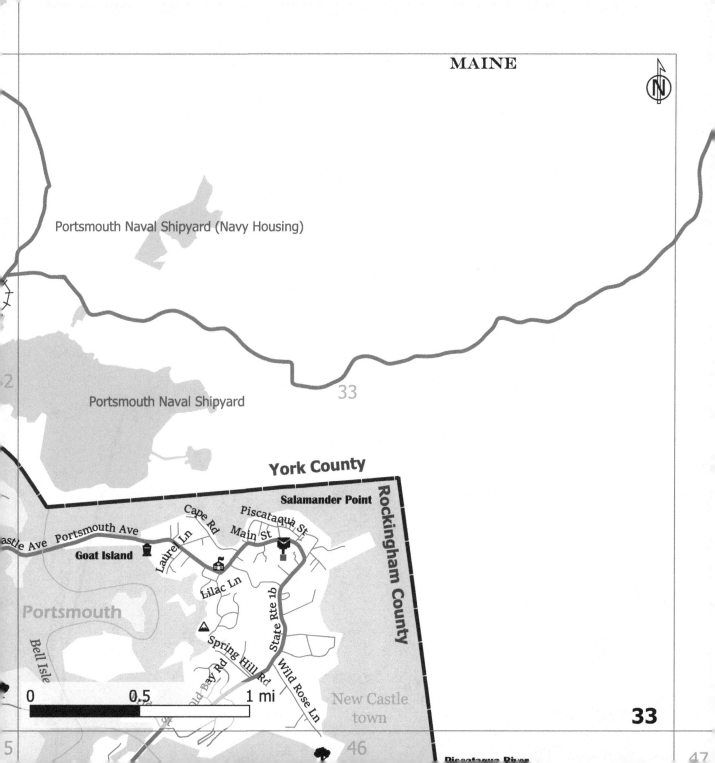

MAINE

Portsmouth Naval Shipyard (Navy Housing)

33

Portsmouth Naval Shipyard

York County

Salamander Point

Piscataqua St

Cape Rd

Main St

Laurel Ln

Goat Island

Portsmouth Ave

astle Ave

Lilac Ln

Portsmouth

State Rte 1b

Rockingham County

Bell Isle

Spring Hill Rd

Old Bay Rd

Wild Rose Ln

New Castle town

0   0.5   1 mi

5

46

33

47

Piscataqua River

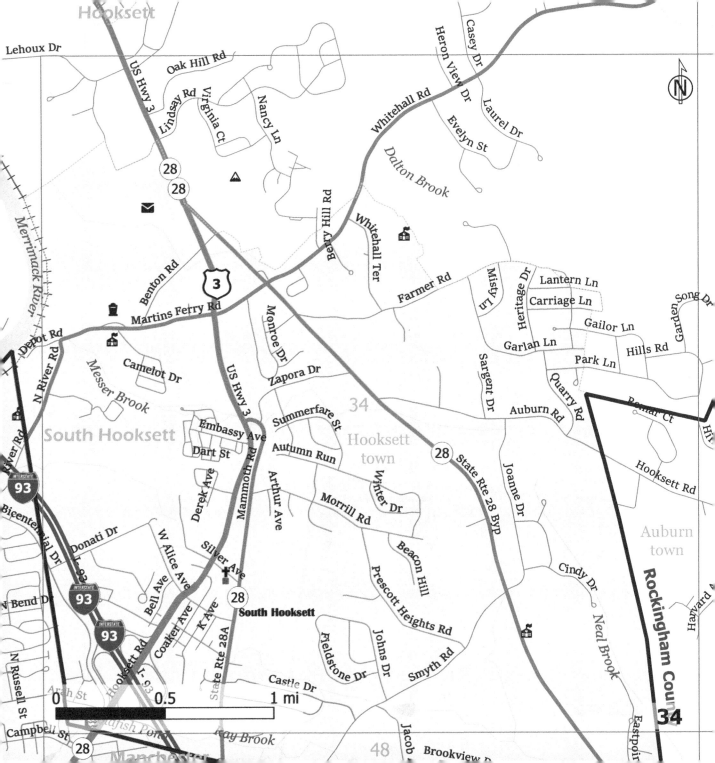

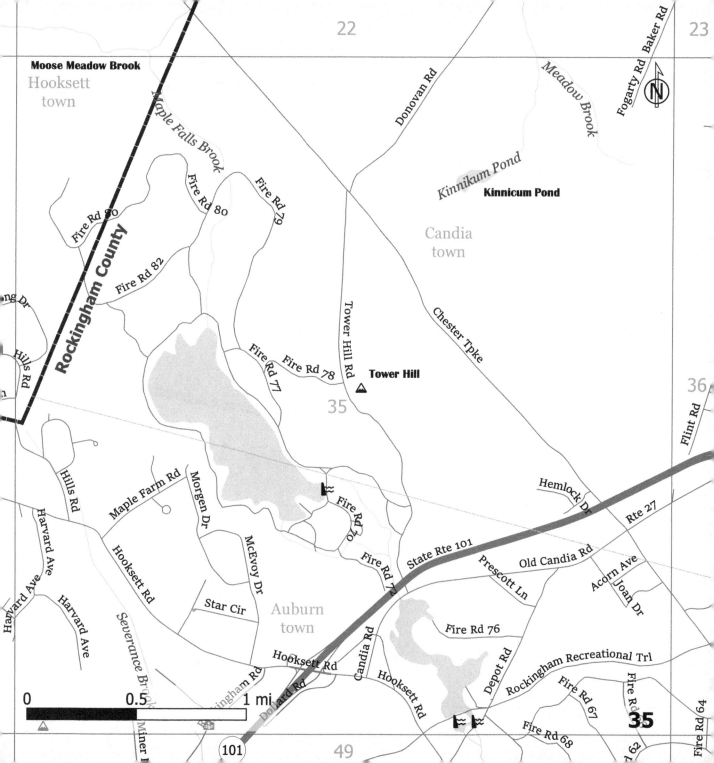

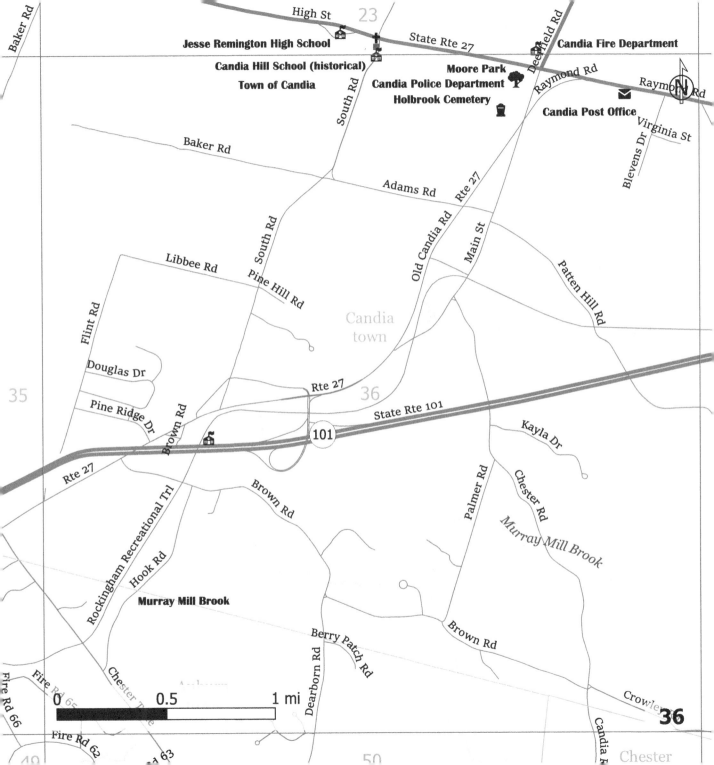

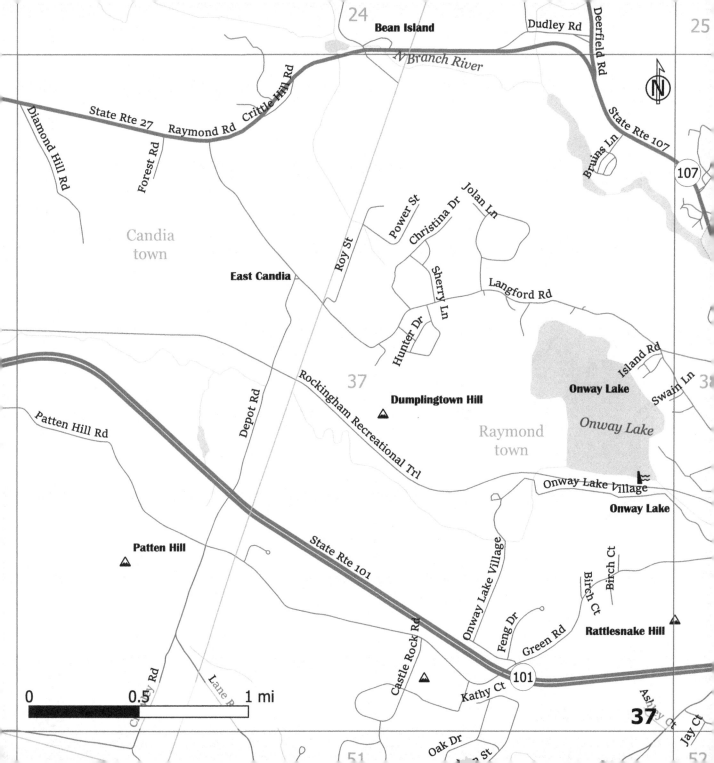

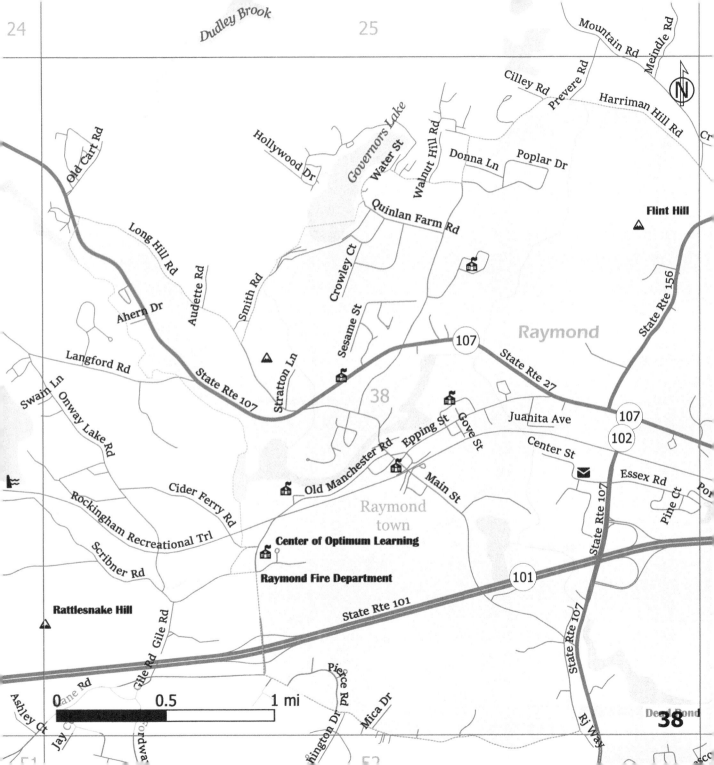

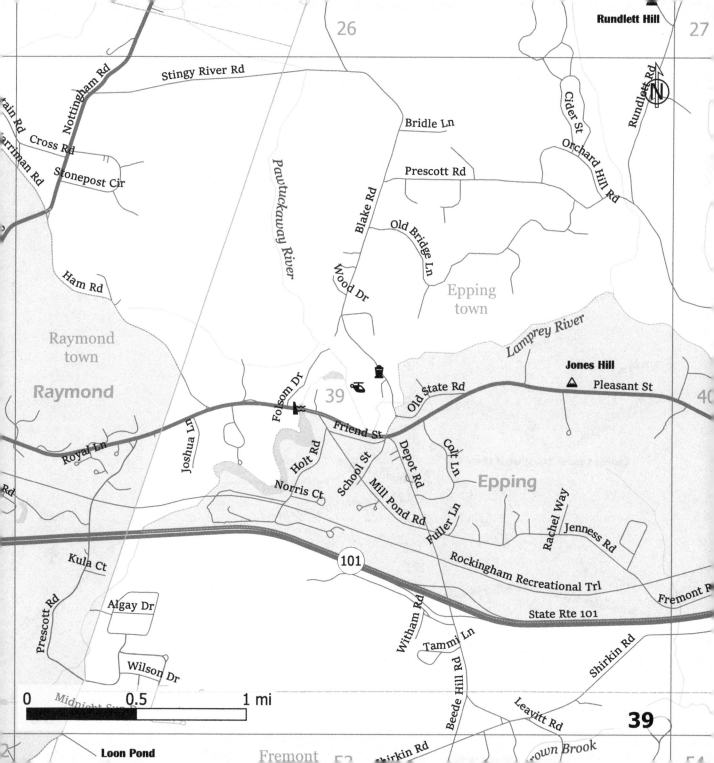

Rundlett Hill

Rundlett Rd

Stingy River Rd

Nottingham Rd

Cross Rd

Stonepost Cir

Harriman Rd

ain Rd

Cider St

Orchard Hill Rd

Bridle Ln

Prescott Rd

Blake Rd

Old Bridge Ln

Pawtuckaway River

Wood Dr

Epping town

Ham Rd

Raymond town

Lamprey River

Raymond

Folsom Dr

39

Old State Rd

Jones Hill

Pleasant St

40

Joshua Ln

Friend St

Royal Ln

Holt Rd

School St

Depot Rd

Colt Ln

Epping

Norris Ct

Mill Pond Rd

Fuller Ln

Rachel Way

Jenness Rd

Rd

Kula Ct

101

Rockingham Recreational Trl

Fremont R

Prescott Rd

Algay Dr

Witham Rd

State Rte 101

Wilson Dr

Tammi Ln

Shirkin Rd

0   0.5   1 mi

Midnight Sun

Beede Hill Rd

Leavitt Rd

39

Loon Pond

Fremont   53   hirkin Rd   rown Brook

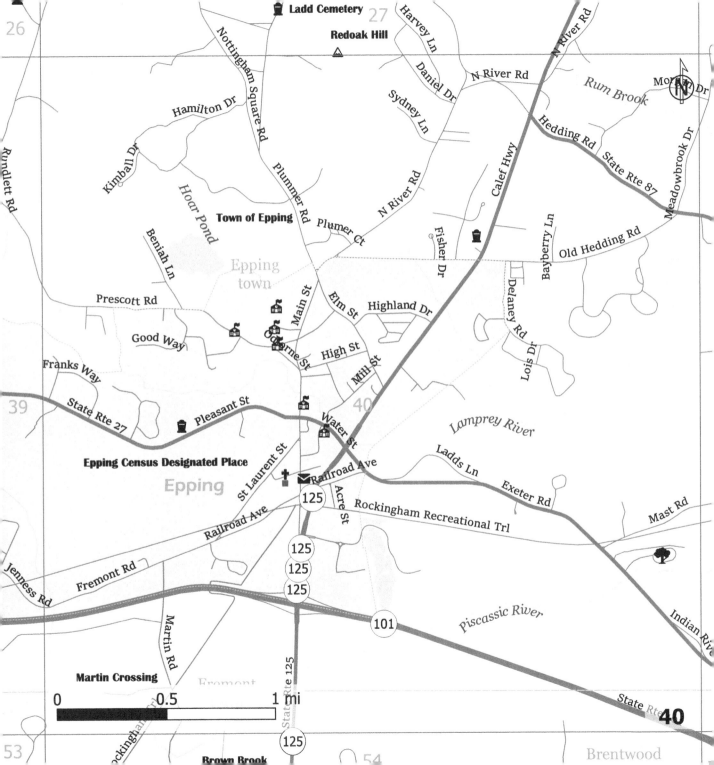

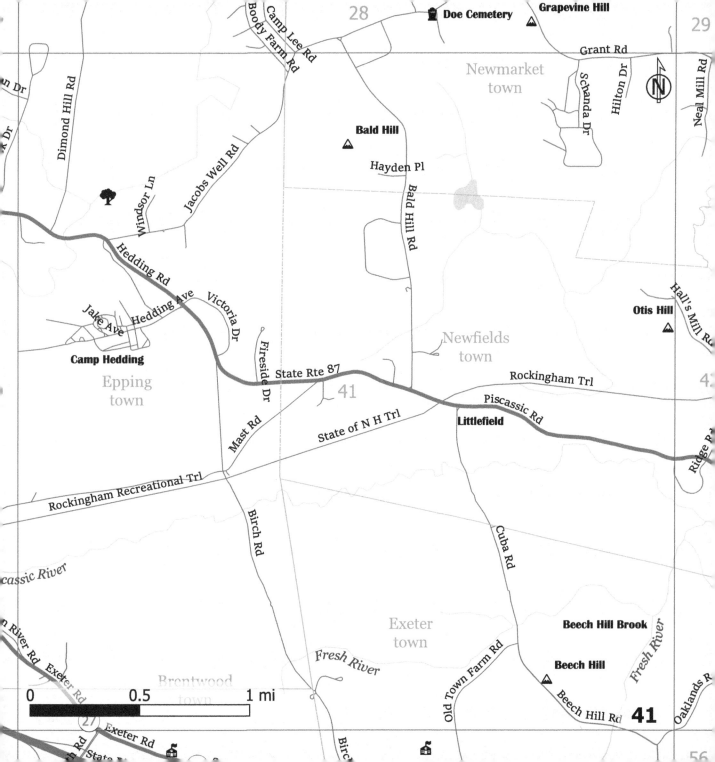

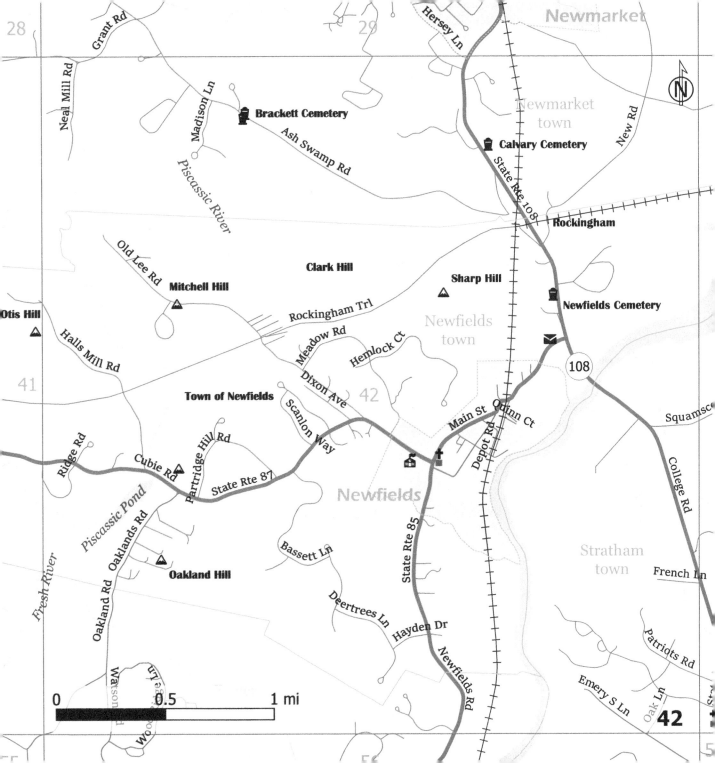

28

29

Newmarket

Hersey Ln

Neal Mill Rd

Grant Rd

Madison Ln

Brackett Cemetery

Ash Swamp Rd

Piscassic River

Newmarket town

New Rd

State Rte 108

Calvary Cemetery

Rockingham

Old Lee Rd

Clark Hill

Sharp Hill

Newfields Cemetery

Mitchell Hill

Otis Hill

Halls Mill Rd

Rockingham Trl

Meadow Rd

Newfields town

108

41

Town of Newfields

Dixon Ave

Hemlock Ct

42

Squamsc

Scanlon Way

Ridge Rd

Cubie Rd

Partridge Hill Rd

State Rte 87

Main St

Quinn Ct

Depot Rd

College Rd

Piscassic Pond

Oaklands Rd

Newfields

Stratham town

French Ln

Fresh River

Oakland Rd

Bassett Ln

State Rte 85

Oakland Hill

Deertrees Ln

Hayden Dr

Newfields Rd

Patriots Rd

Watson

Emery S Ln

Oak Ln

42

0   0.5   1 mi

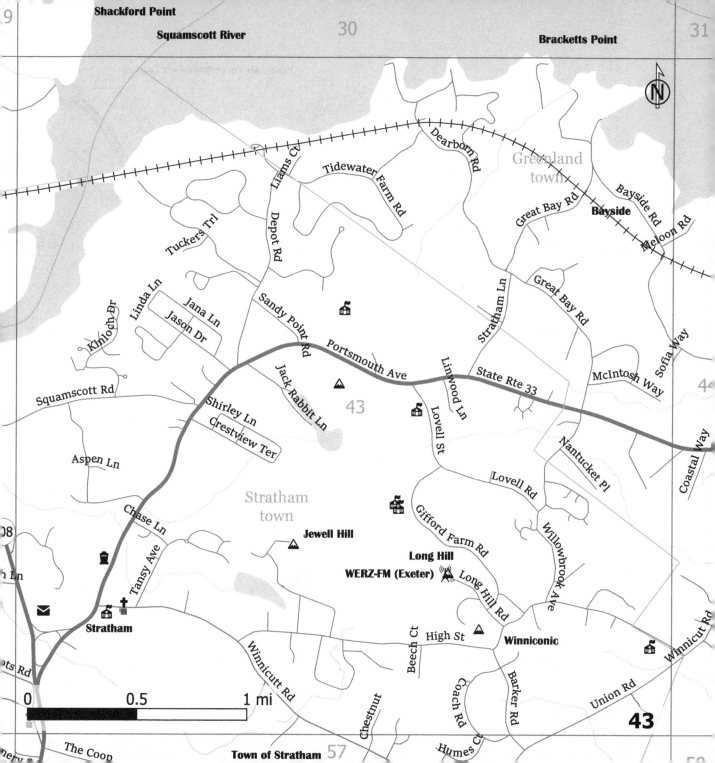

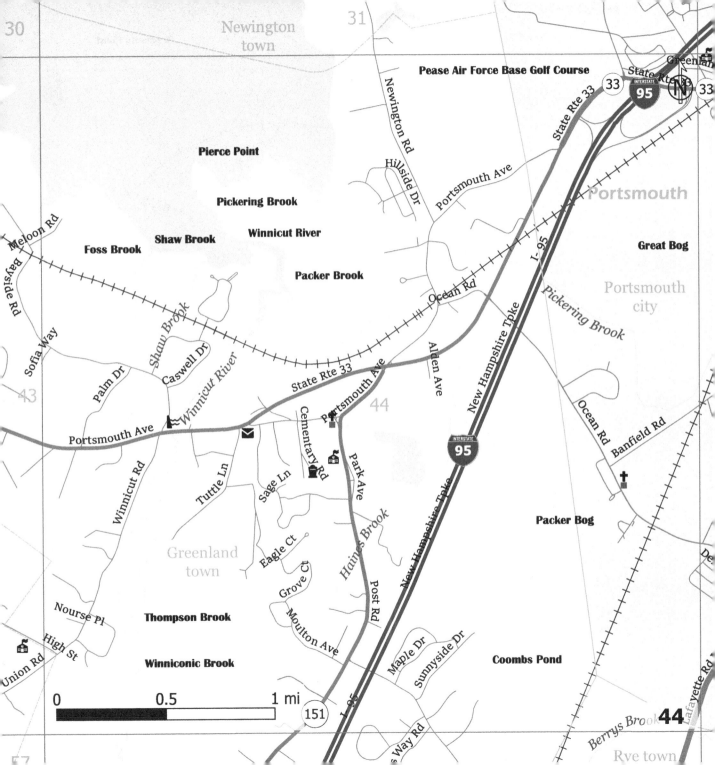

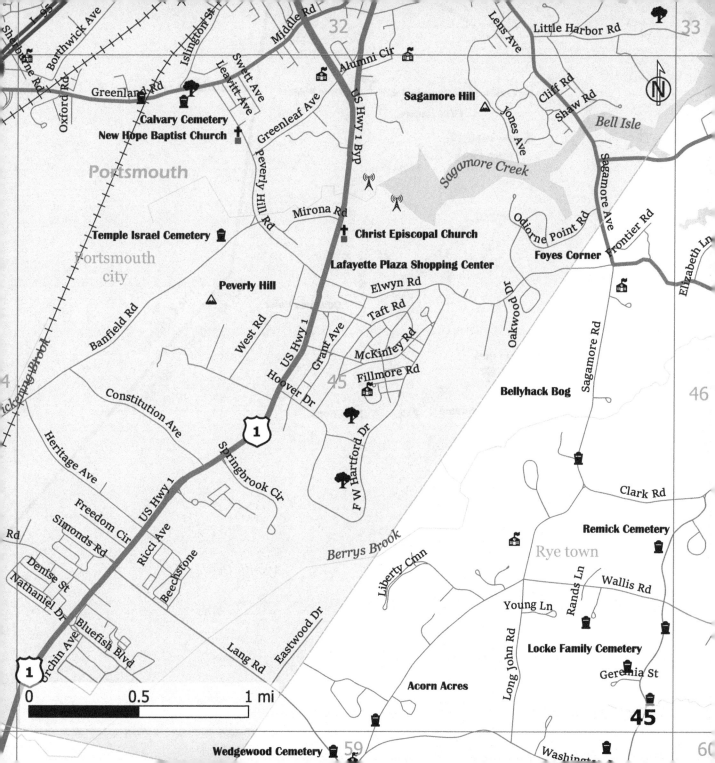

Little Harbor Rd

Lens Ave

Borthwick Ave

I-95

Shelburne Rd

Oxford Rd

Islington St

Swett Ave

Leavitt Ave

Middle Rd

Alumni Cir

Sagamore Hill

Jones Ave

Cliff Rd

Shaw Rd

Bell Isle

Greenland Rd

Calvary Cemetery

New Hope Baptist Church

Greenleaf Ave

Peverly Hill Rd

Sagamore Creek

Portsmouth

US Hwy 1 Byp

Odiorne Point Dr

Sagamore Ave

Temple Israel Cemetery

Portsmouth city

Mirona Rd

Christ Episcopal Church

Foyes Corner

Frontier Rd

Elizabeth Ln

Lafayette Plaza Shopping Center

Elwyn Rd

Peverly Hill

West Rd

Taft Rd

Oakwood Dr

Banfield Rd

US Hwy 1

Grant Ave

McKinley Rd

Fillmore Rd

Sagamore Rd

Bellyhack Bog

46

4

Pickering Brook

Constitution Ave

Hoover Dr

45

F W Hartford Dr

Heritage Ave

1

Springbrook Cir

Clark Rd

Freedom Cir

US Hwy 1

Remick Cemetery

Rd

Simonds Rd

Ricci Ave

Beechstone

Berrys Brook

Liberty Cmn

Rye town

Rands Ln

Wallis Rd

Denise St

Nathaniel Dr

Young Ln

Long John Rd

1

Orchin Ave

Bluefish Blvd

Lang Rd

Eastwood Dr

Locke Family Cemetery

Geremia St

Acorn Acres

45

0   0.5   1 mi

N

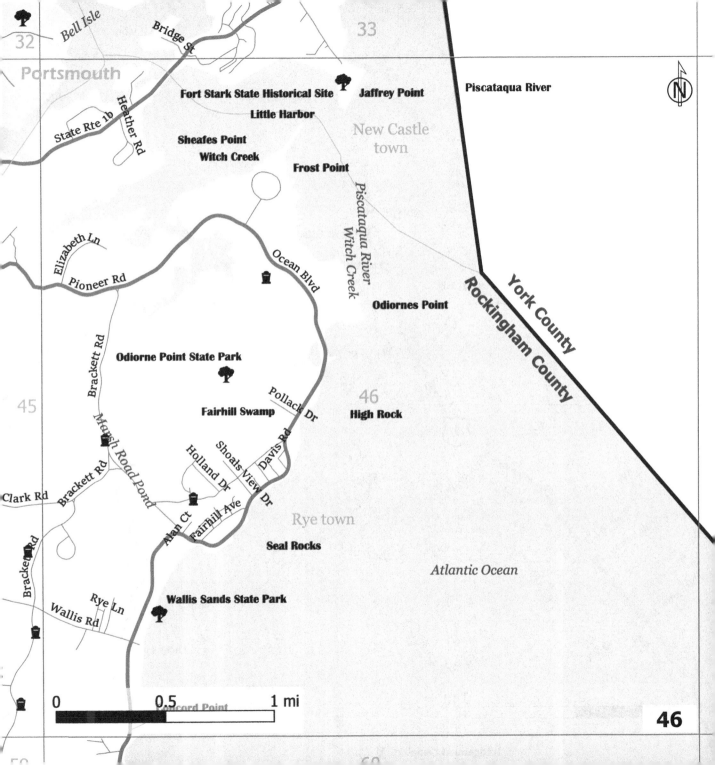

Bell Isle

Bridge St

Portsmouth

State Rte 1b

Heather Rd

Fort Stark State Historical Site

Jaffrey Point

Piscataqua River

Little Harbor

New Castle
town

Sheafes Point

Witch Creek

Frost Point

Piscataqua River
Witch Creek

Elizabeth Ln

Ocean Blvd

Pioneer Rd

Odiornes Point

York County

Rockingham County

Brackett Rd

Odiorne Point State Park

46

Pollack Dr

High Rock

45

Fairhill Swamp

Marsh Road Pond

Davis Rd

Shoals View Dr

Clark Rd

Holland Dr

Brackett Rd

Alan Ct

Fairhill Ave

Rye town

Brackett Rd

Seal Rocks

Atlantic Ocean

Rye Ln

Wallis Sands State Park

Wallis Rd

0   0.5   1 mi

Concord Point

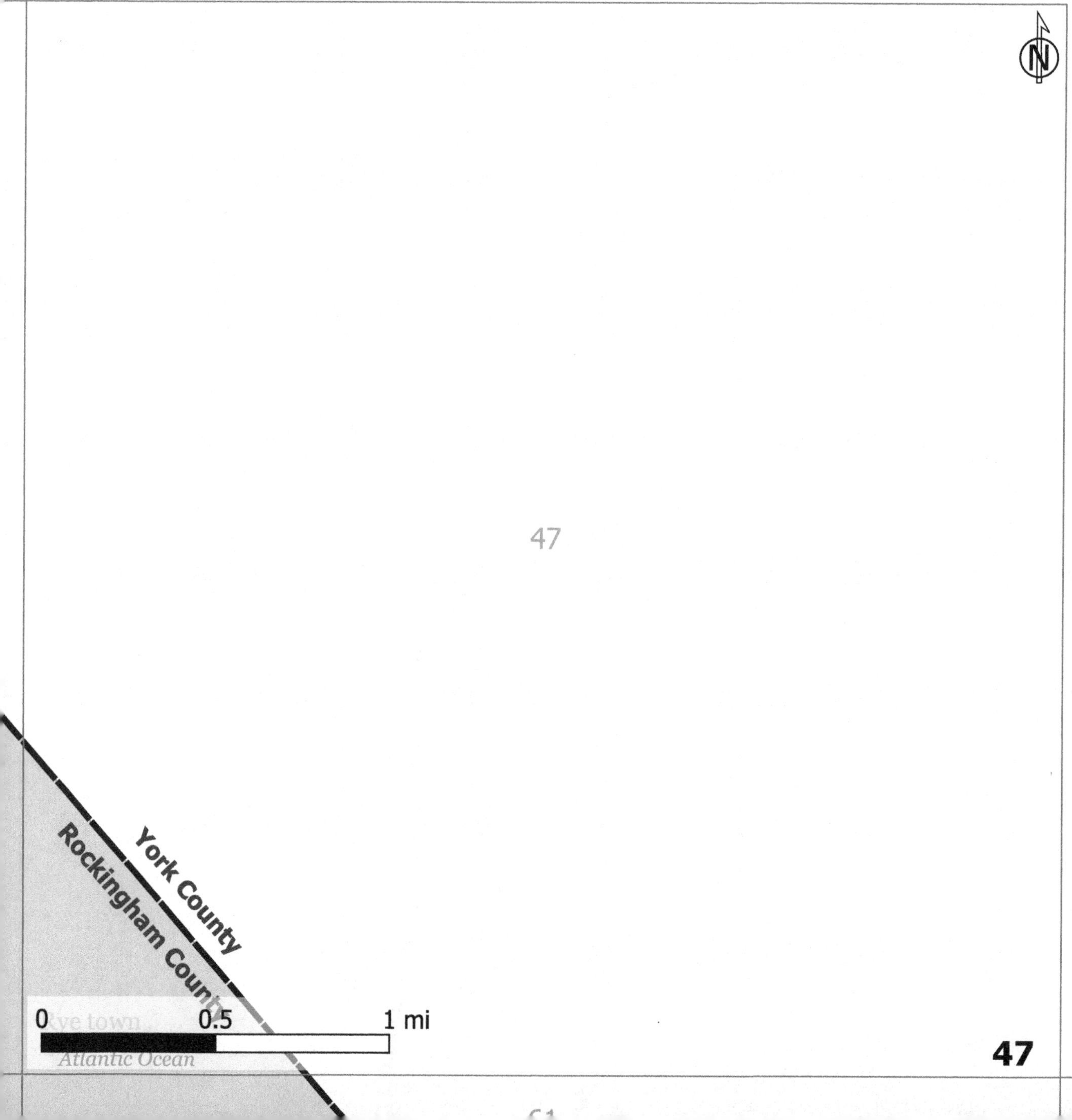

47

York County

Rockingham County

ye town

Atlantic Ocean

0   0.5   1 mi

47

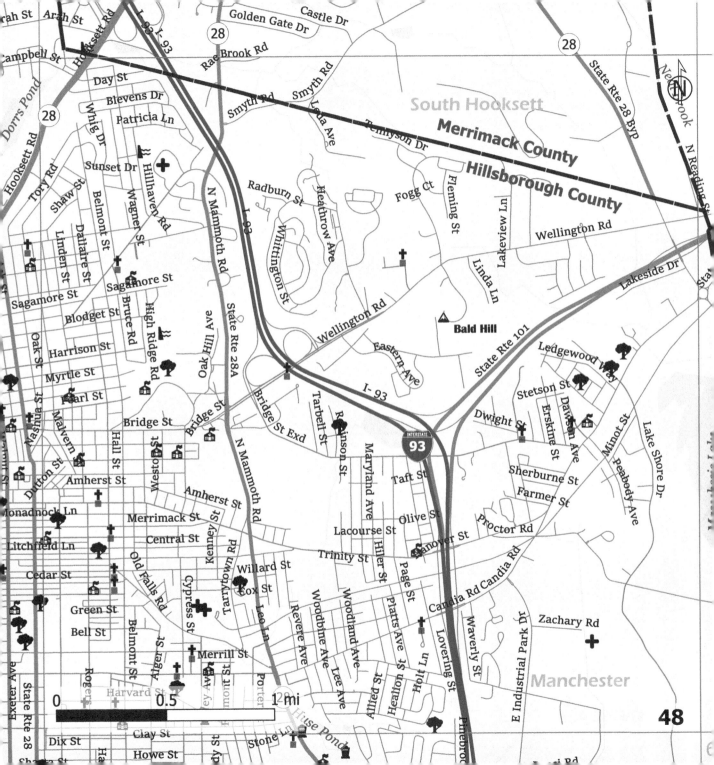

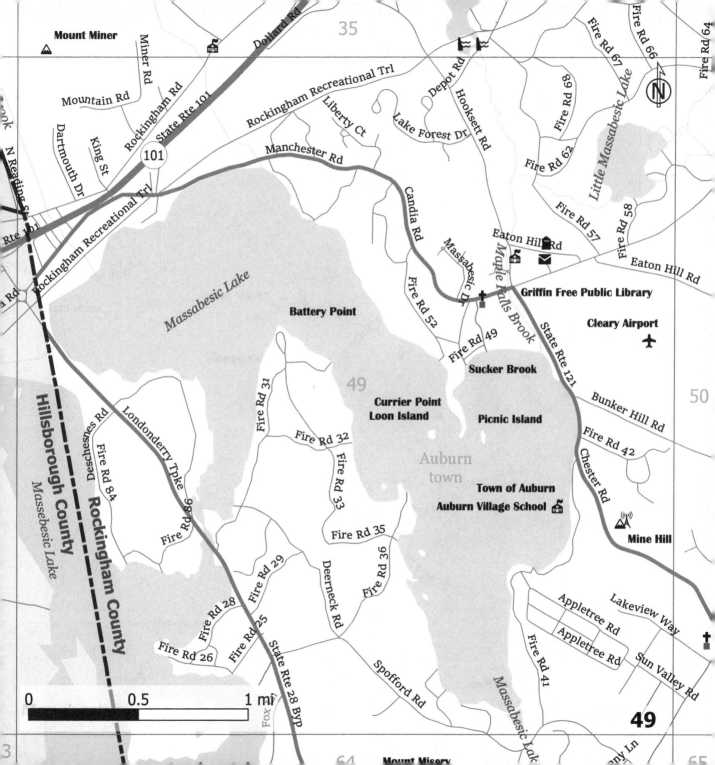

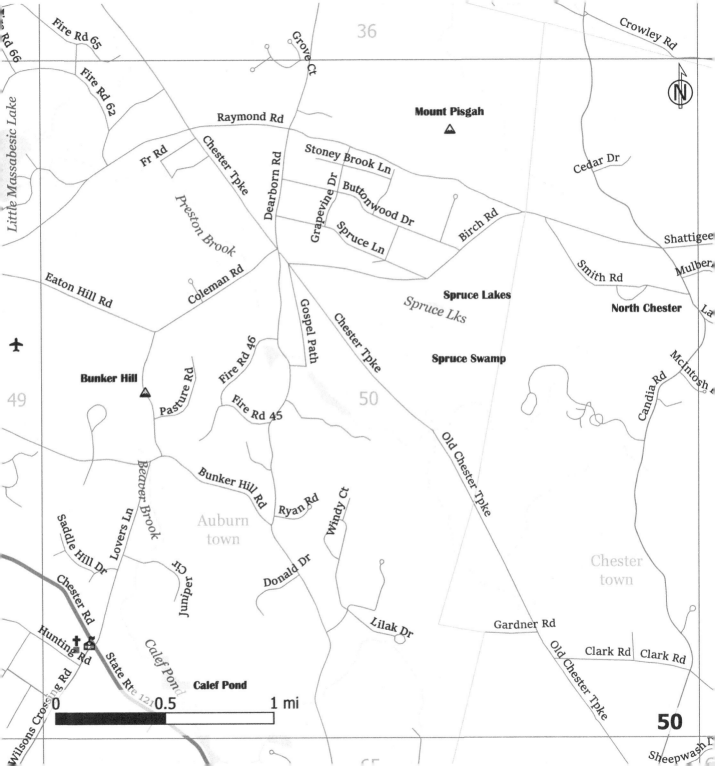

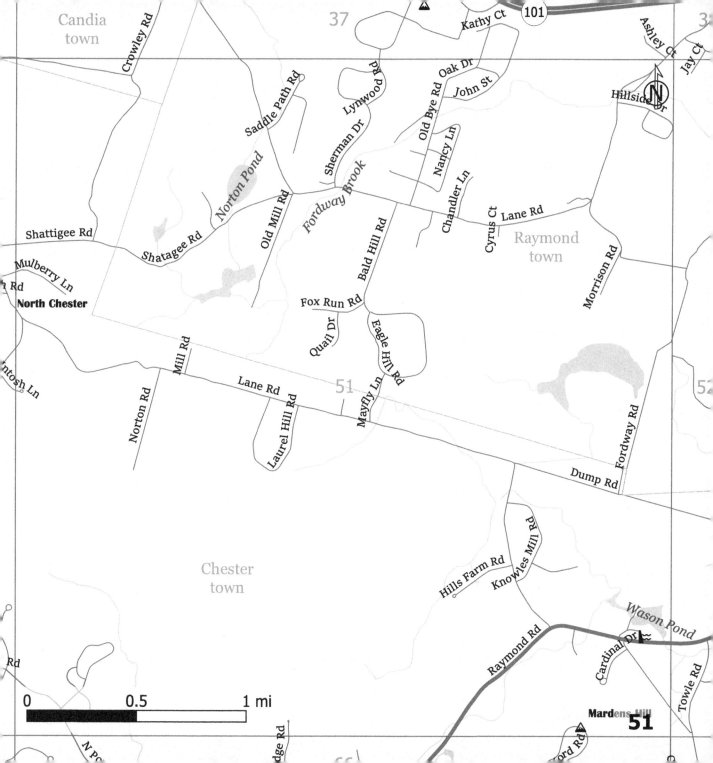

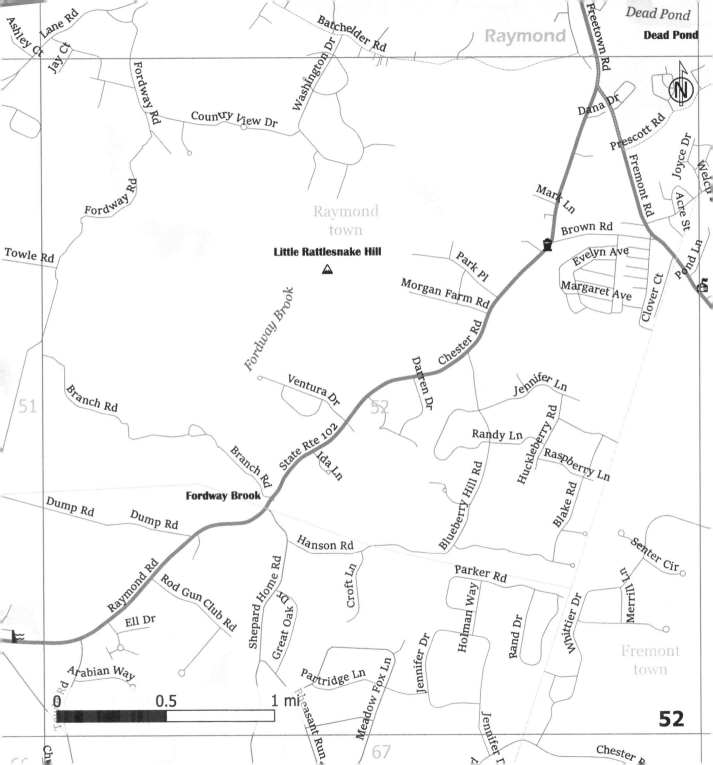

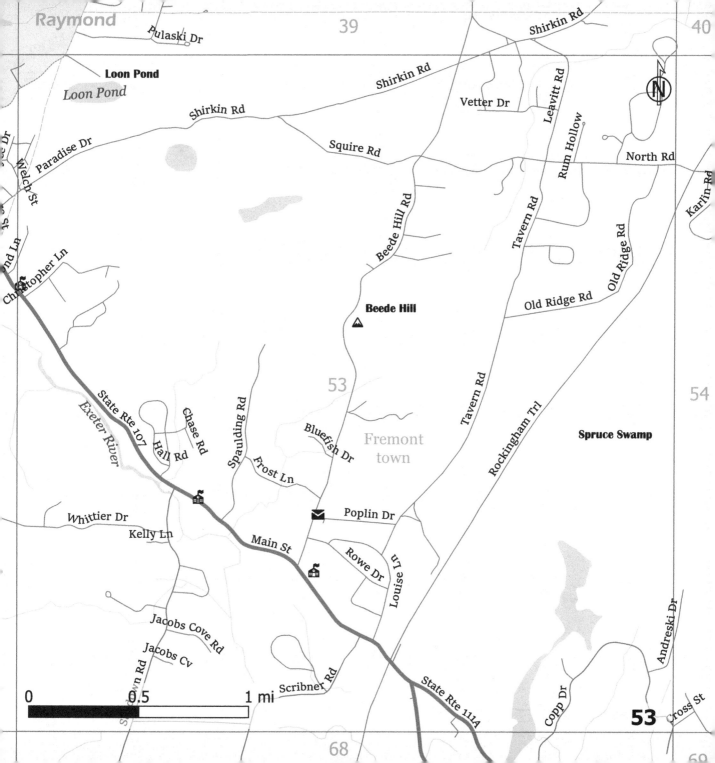

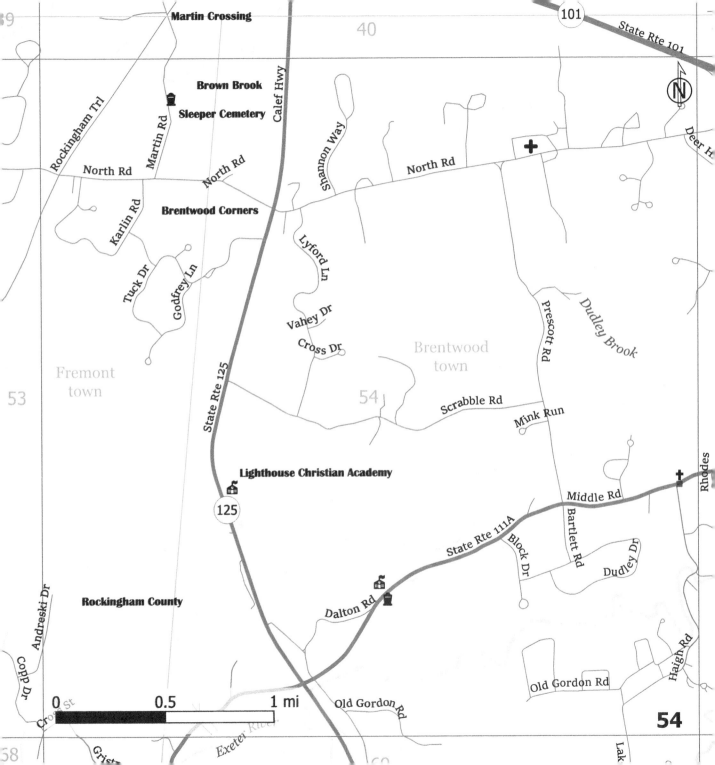

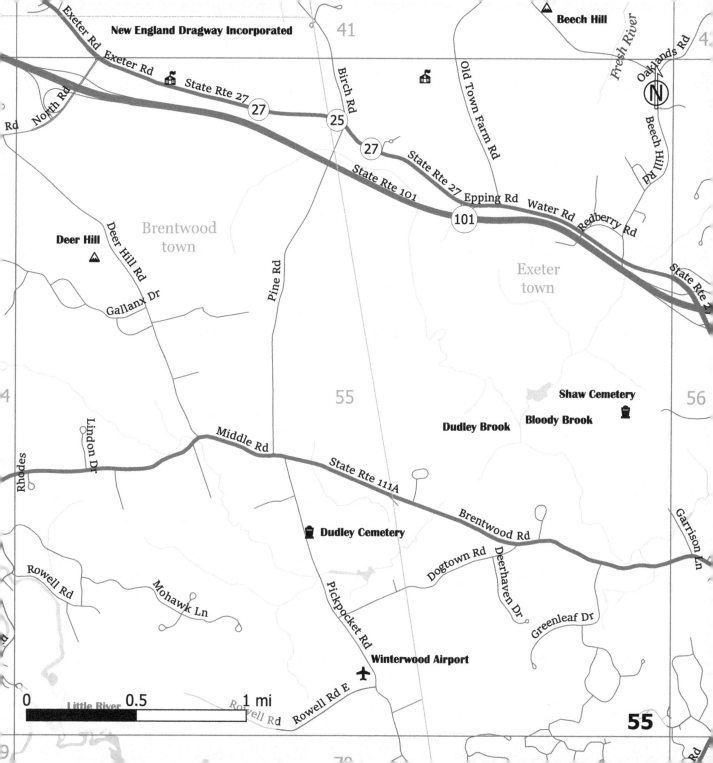

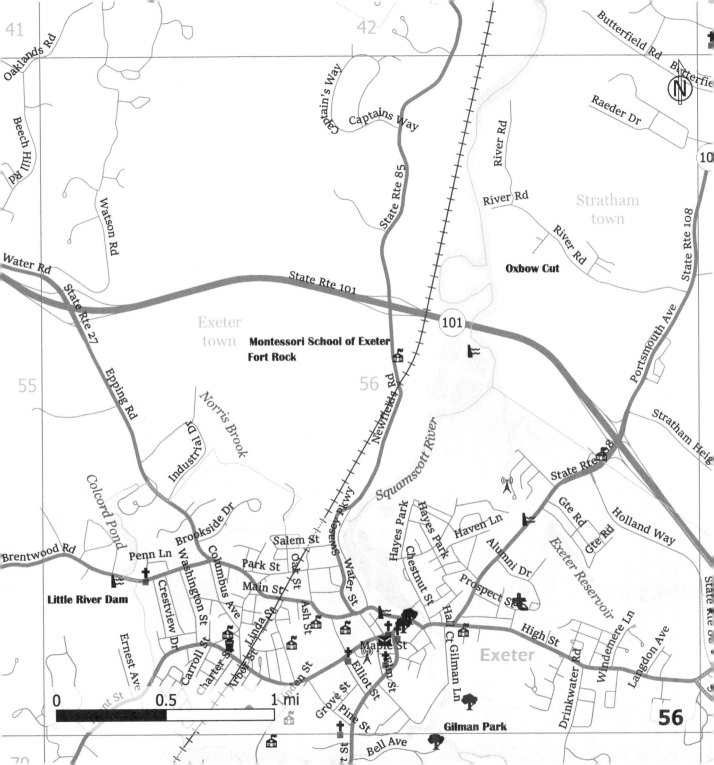

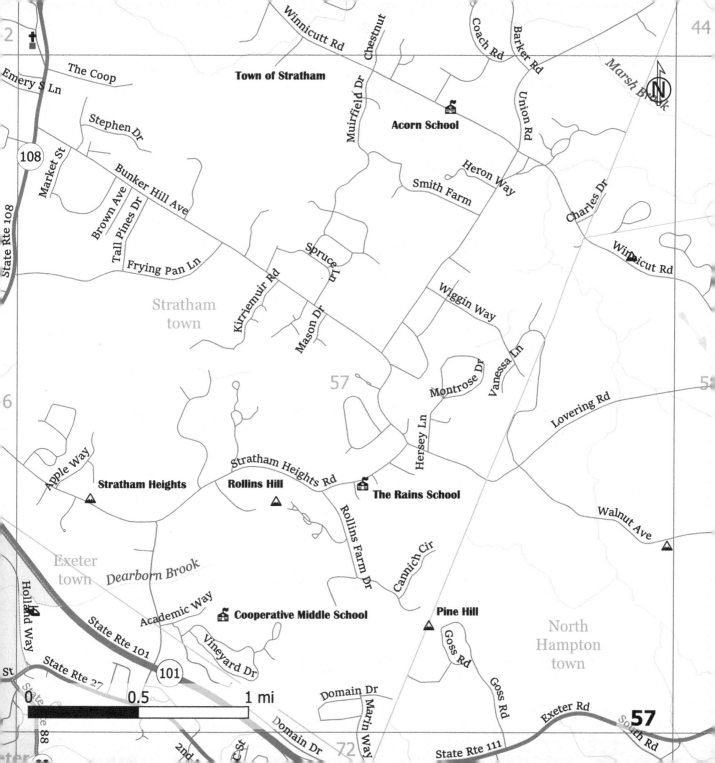

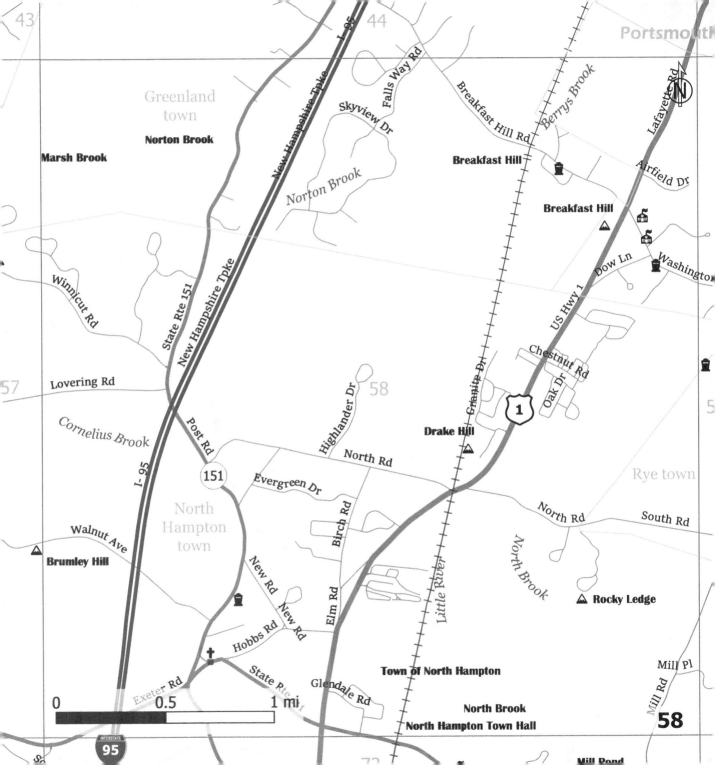

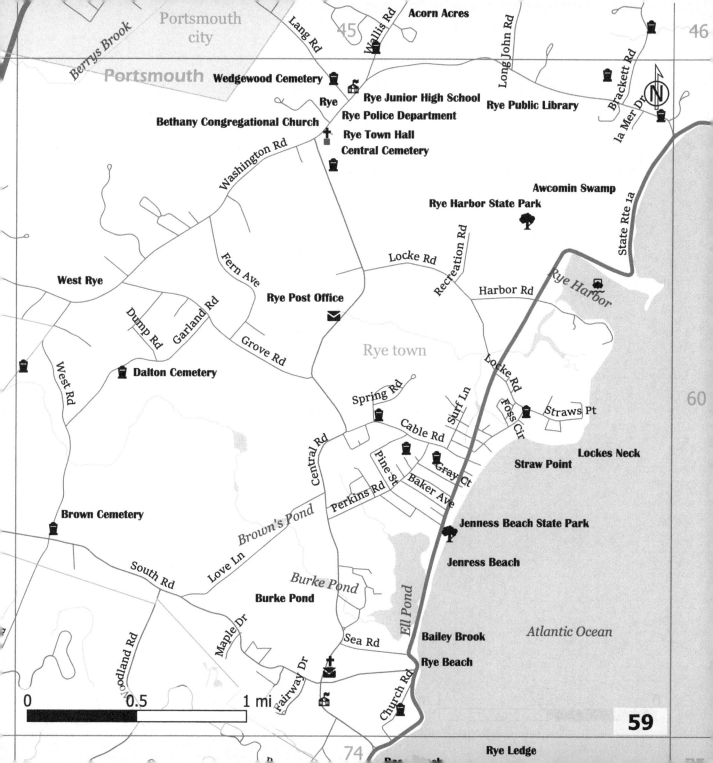

Concord Point

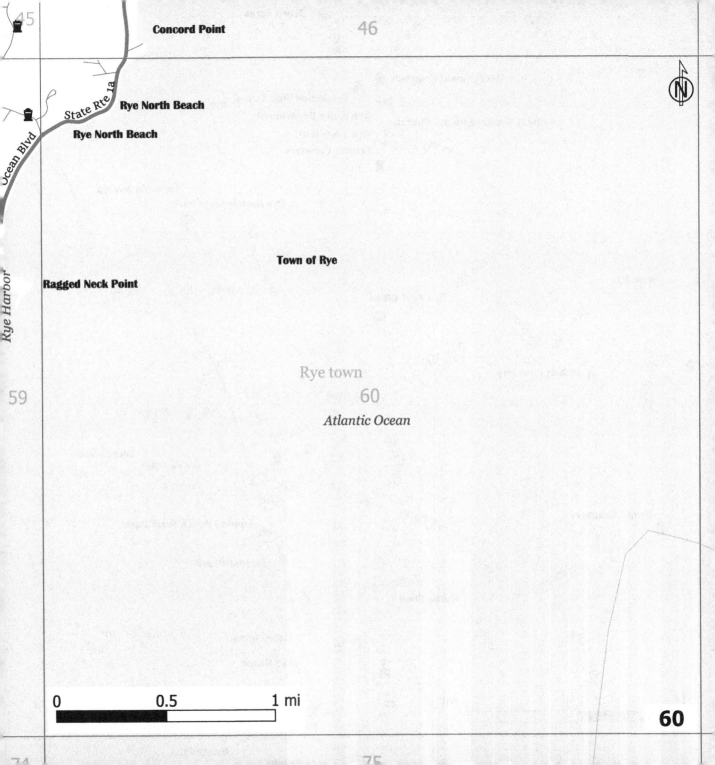

State Rte 1a

Ocean Blvd

Rye North Beach

Rye North Beach

Rye Harbor

Town of Rye

Ragged Neck Point

Rye town

60

Atlantic Ocean

N

0   0.5   1 mi

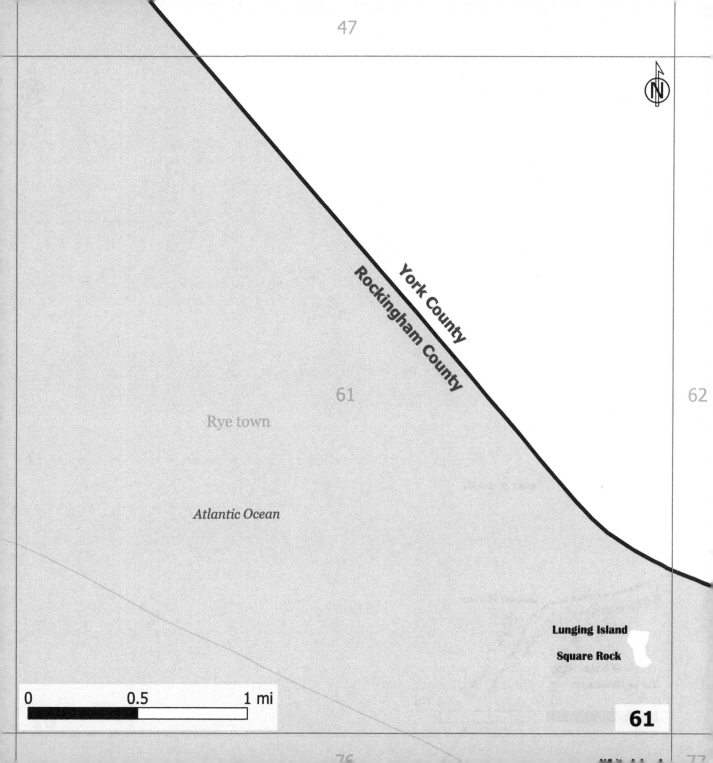

47

York County

Rockingham County

62

61

Rye town

Atlantic Ocean

Lunging Island

Square Rock

0   0.5   1 mi

61

76   77

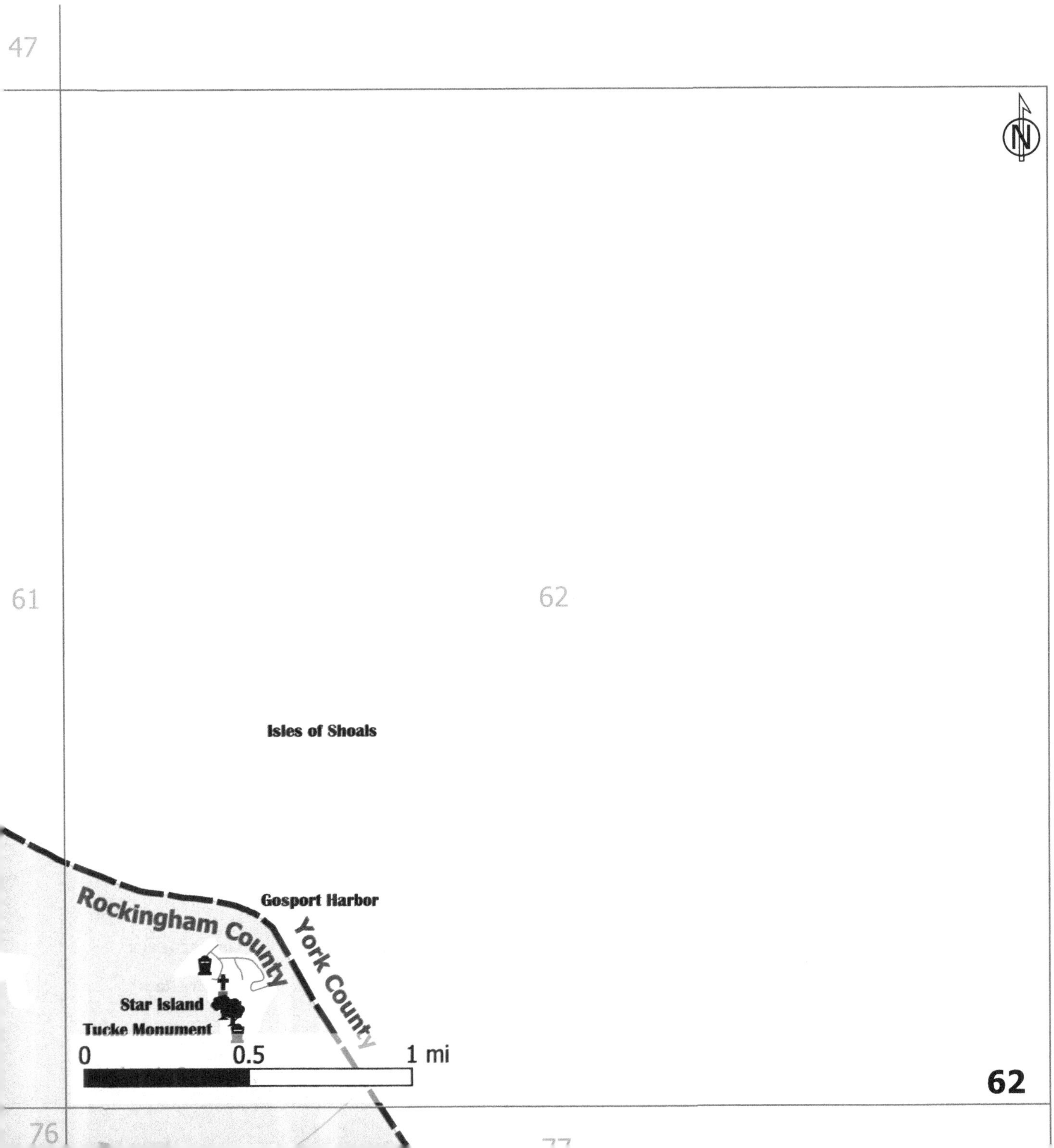

N

61   62

Isles of Shoals

Rockingham County

York County

Gosport Harbor

Star Island

Tucke Monument

0   0.5   1 mi

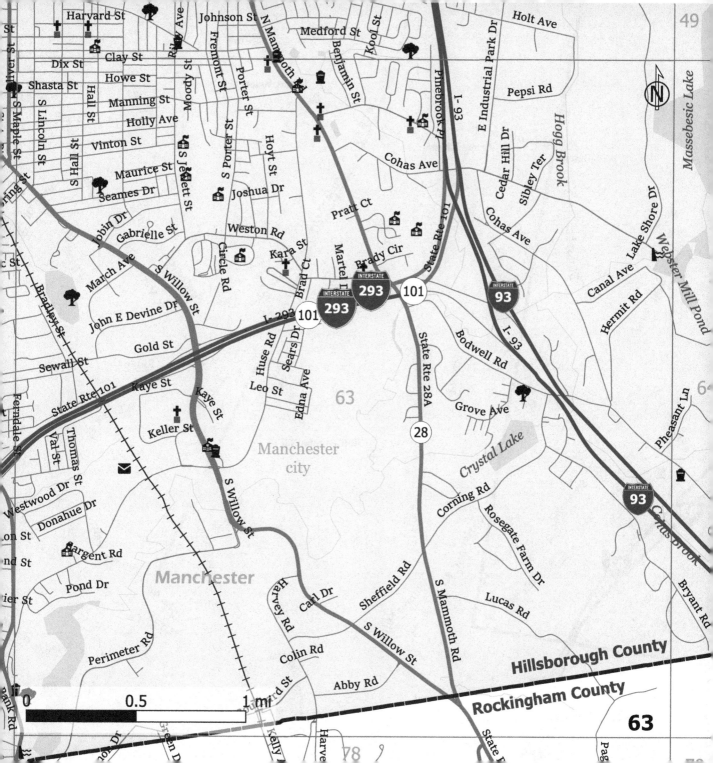

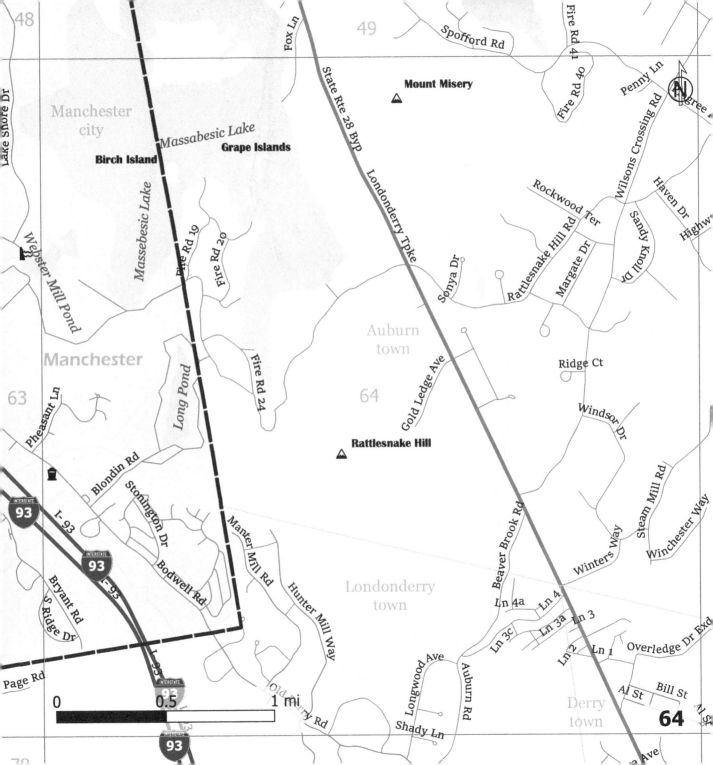

48

49

Spofford Rd

Fire Rd 41

Fire Rd 40

Penny Ln

N

Mount Misery

State Rte 28 Byp

Londonderry Tpke

Manchester city

Massabesic Lake

Grape Islands

Birch Island

Massebesic Lake

Lake Shore Dr

Wilsons Crossing Rd

Haven Dr

Highw

Rockwood Ter

Sandy Knoll Dr

Margate Dr

Rattlesnake Hill Rd

Sonya Dr

Webster Mill Pond

Fire Rd 19

Fire Rd 20

Fire Rd 24

Auburn town

Gold Ledge Ave

Ridge Ct

64

Manchester

63

Long Pond

Rattlesnake Hill

Windsor Dr

Pheasant Ln

Steam Mill Rd

Winchester Way

Blondin Rd

INTERSTATE 93

Stonington Dr

Bodwell Rd

Beaver Brook Rd

Winters Way

I-93

INTERSTATE 93

Manter Mill Rd

Ln 4a

Ln 4

Bryant Rd

S Ridge Dr

I-93

Hunter Mill Way

Londonderry town

Ln 3c

Ln 3a

Ln 3

Ln 2

Ln 1

Overledge Dr Exd

Page Rd

0

INTERSTATE 93

0.5

1 mi

Old Derry Rd

Longwood Ave

Auburn Rd

Shady Ln

Al St

Bill St

Al St

Derry town

64

INTERSTATE 93

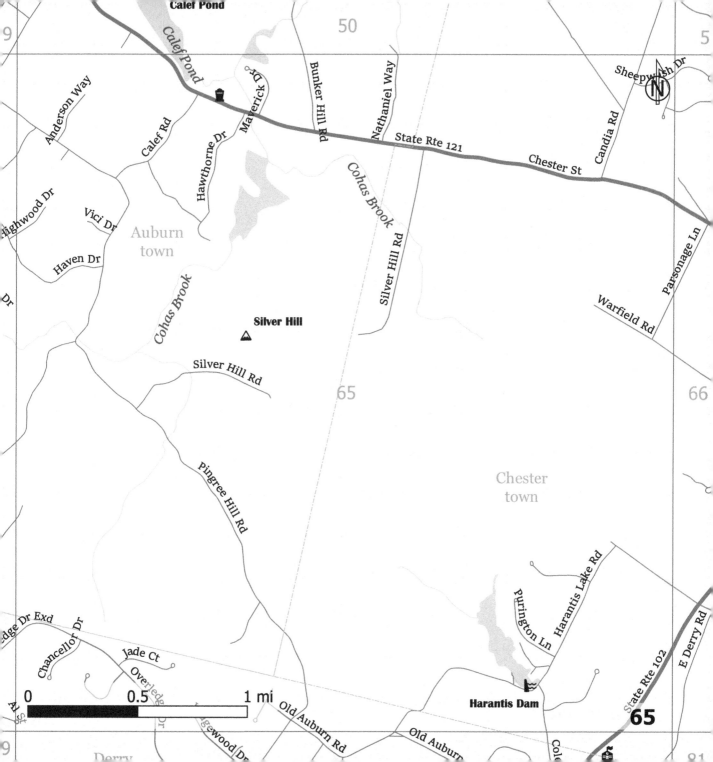

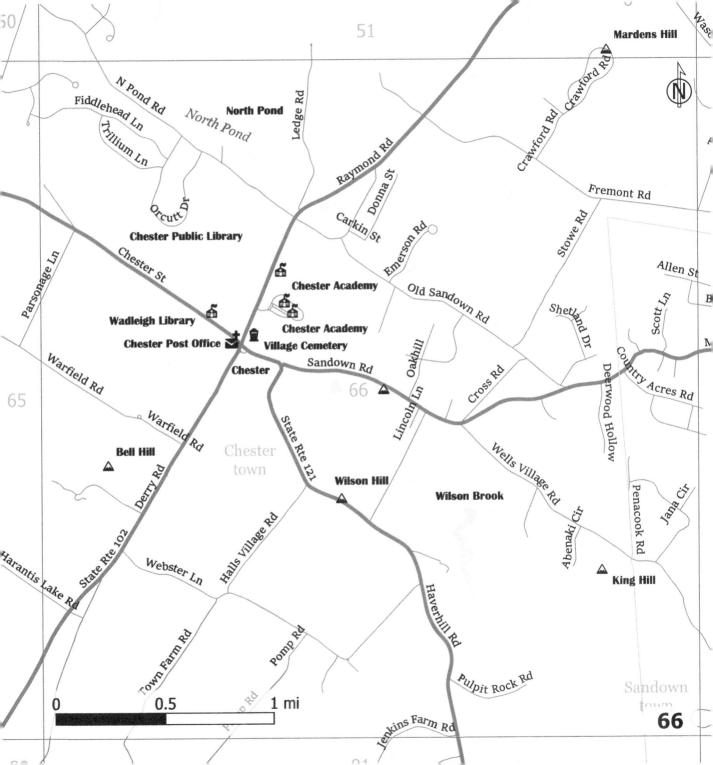

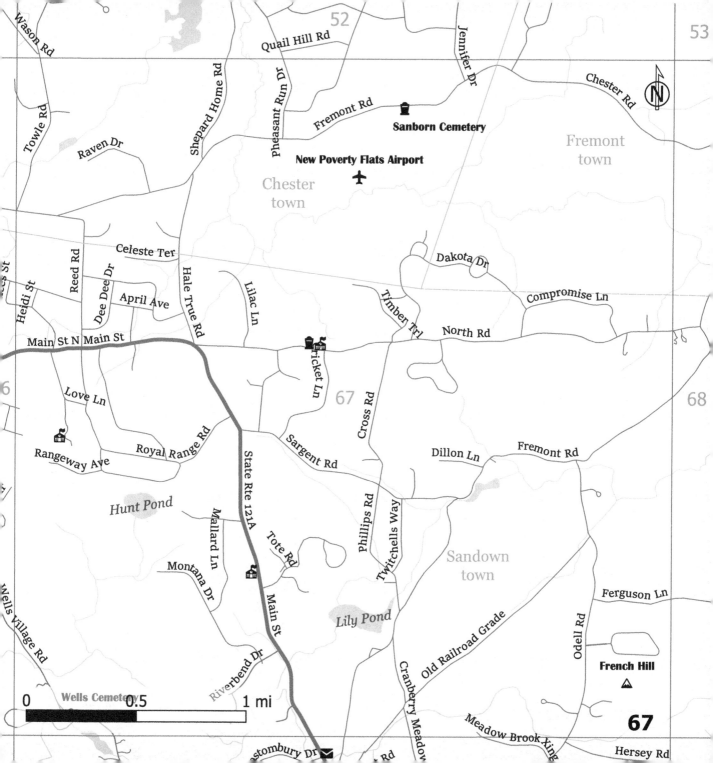

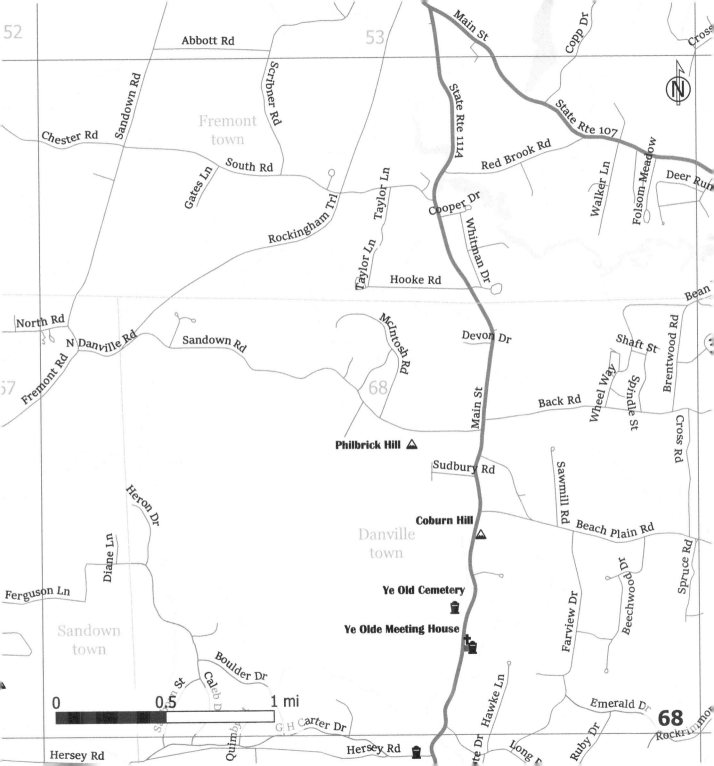

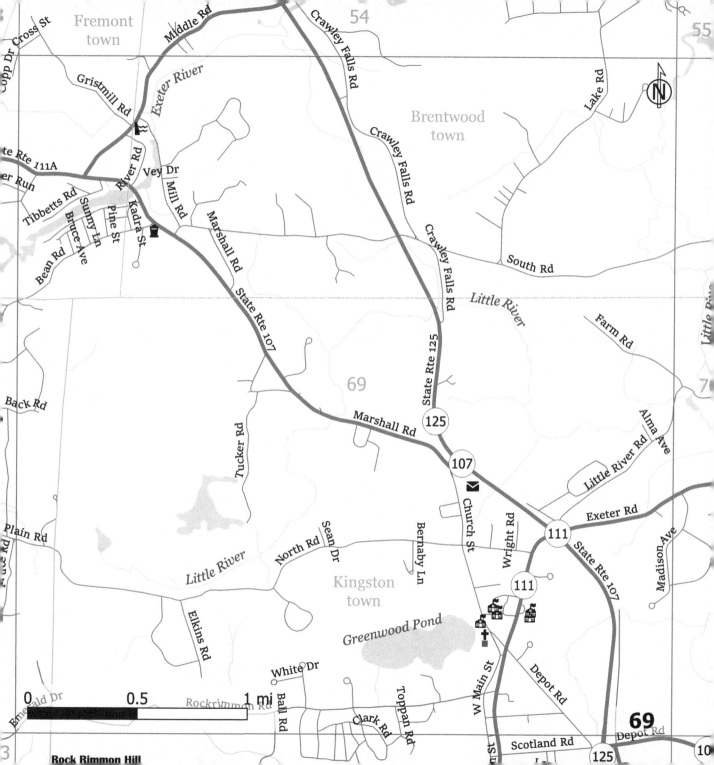

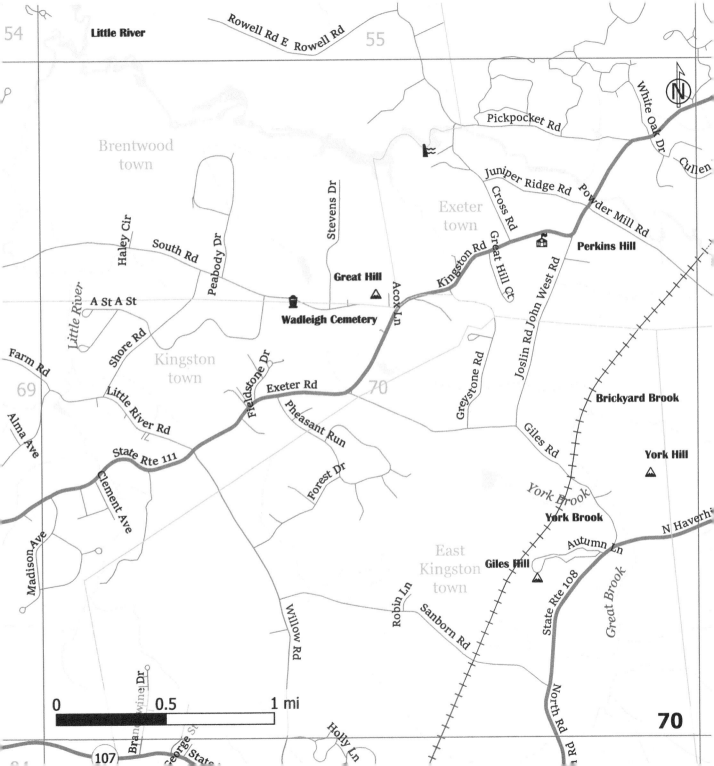

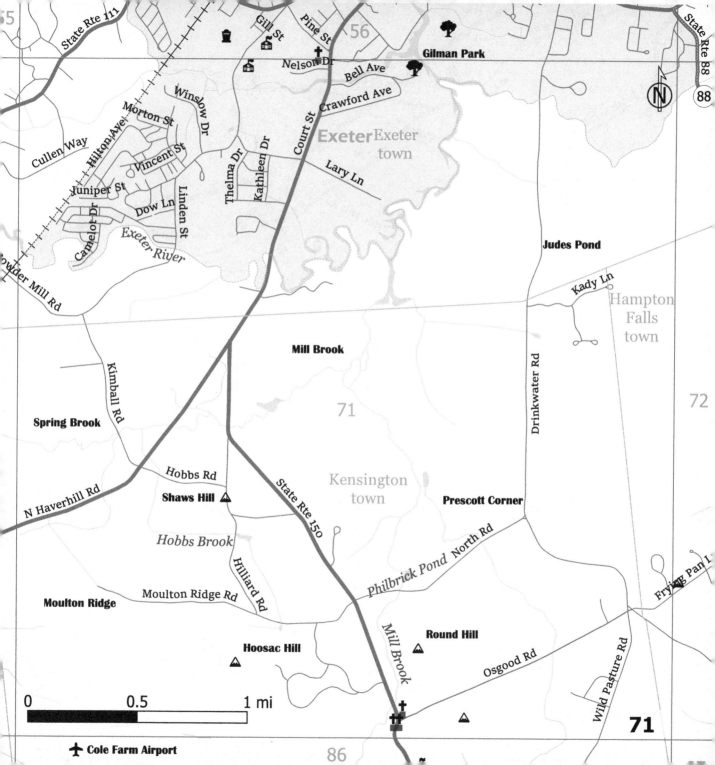

State Rte 11

State Rte 88

56

88

N

Gill St

Pine St

Gilman Park

Nelson Dr

Bell Ave

Crawford Ave

Winslow Dr

Morton St

Court St

Exeter Exeter town

Cullen Way

Hilton Ave

Vincent St

Thelma Dr

Kathleen Dr

Lary Ln

Juniper St

Linden St

Dow Ln

Camelot Dr

Judes Pond

Exeter River

Kady Ln

Powder Mill Rd

Hampton Falls town

72

Mill Brook

Kimball Rd

Drinkwater Rd

71

Spring Brook

Hobbs Rd

Kensington town

N Haverhill Rd

Shaws Hill ⛺

Prescott Corner

Hobbs Brook

Hilliard Rd

State Rte 150

North Rd

Moulton Ridge

Moulton Ridge Rd

Philbrick Pond

Frying Pan L

Hoosac Hill
⛰

Mill Brook

Round Hill
⛰

Osgood Rd

Wild Pasture Rd

71

| 0 | 0.5 | 1 mi |

✈ **Cole Farm Airport**

86

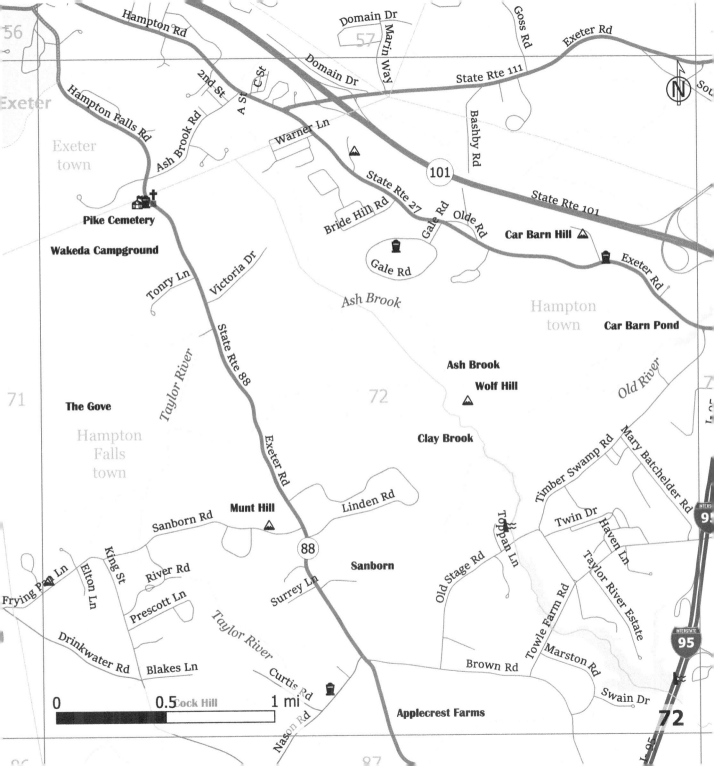

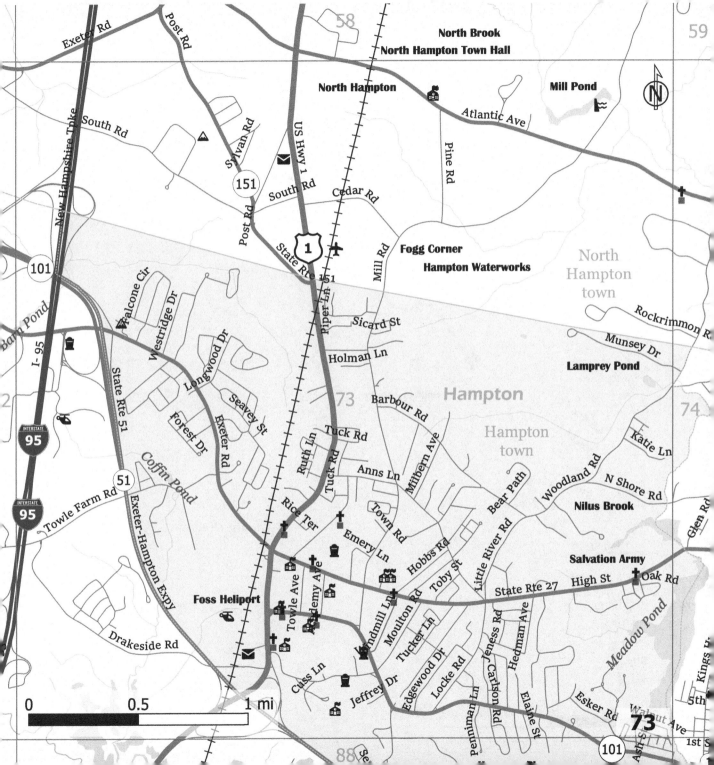

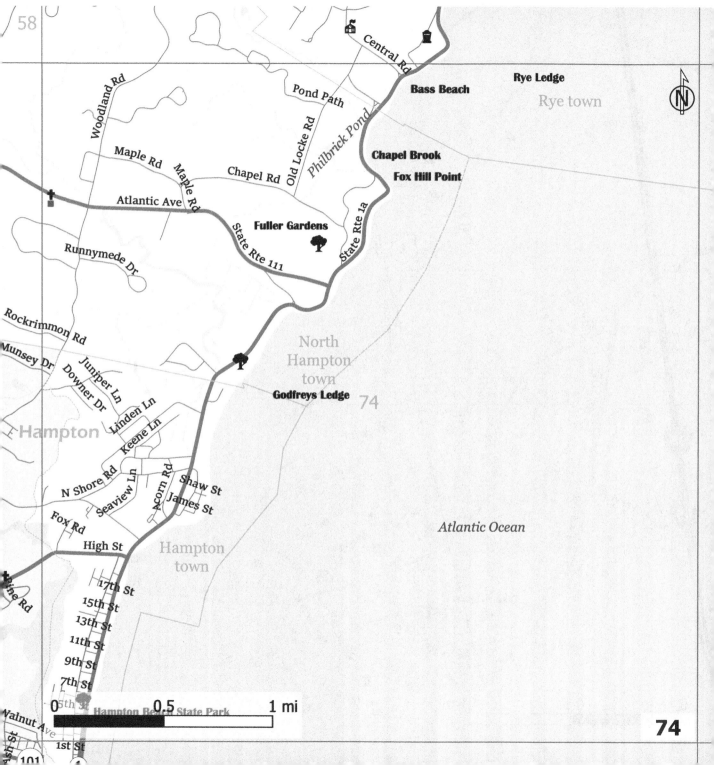

Woodland Rd

Central Rd

Pond Path

Bass Beach

Rye Ledge

Rye town

Maple Rd

Old Locke Rd

Chapel Rd

Philbrick Pond

Chapel Brook

Fox Hill Point

Maple Rd

Atlantic Ave

State Rte 1a

Fuller Gardens

Runnymede Dr

State Rte 111

Rockrimmon Rd

North
Hampton
town

Munsey Dr

Juniper Ln

Downer Dr

Linden Ln

Godfreys Ledge

74

Hampton

Keene Ln

N Shore Rd

Seaview Ln

Acorn Rd

Shaw St

James St

Fox Rd

High St

Hampton
town

Atlantic Ocean

Pine Rd

17th St

15th St

13th St

11th St

9th St

7th St

5th St

Hampton Beach State Park

Walnut Ave

1st St

101

0   0.5   1 mi

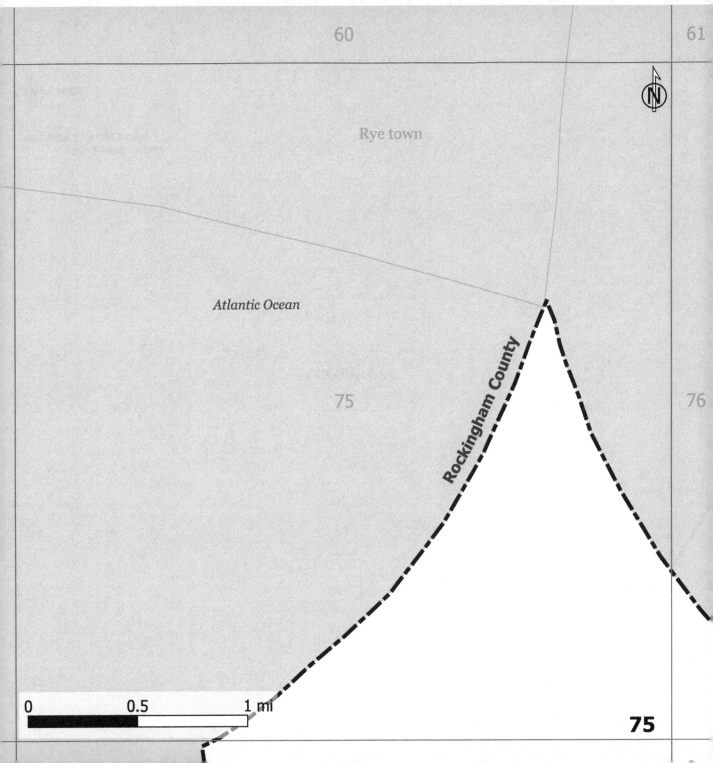

Rye town

Atlantic Ocean

75

Rockingham County

76

75

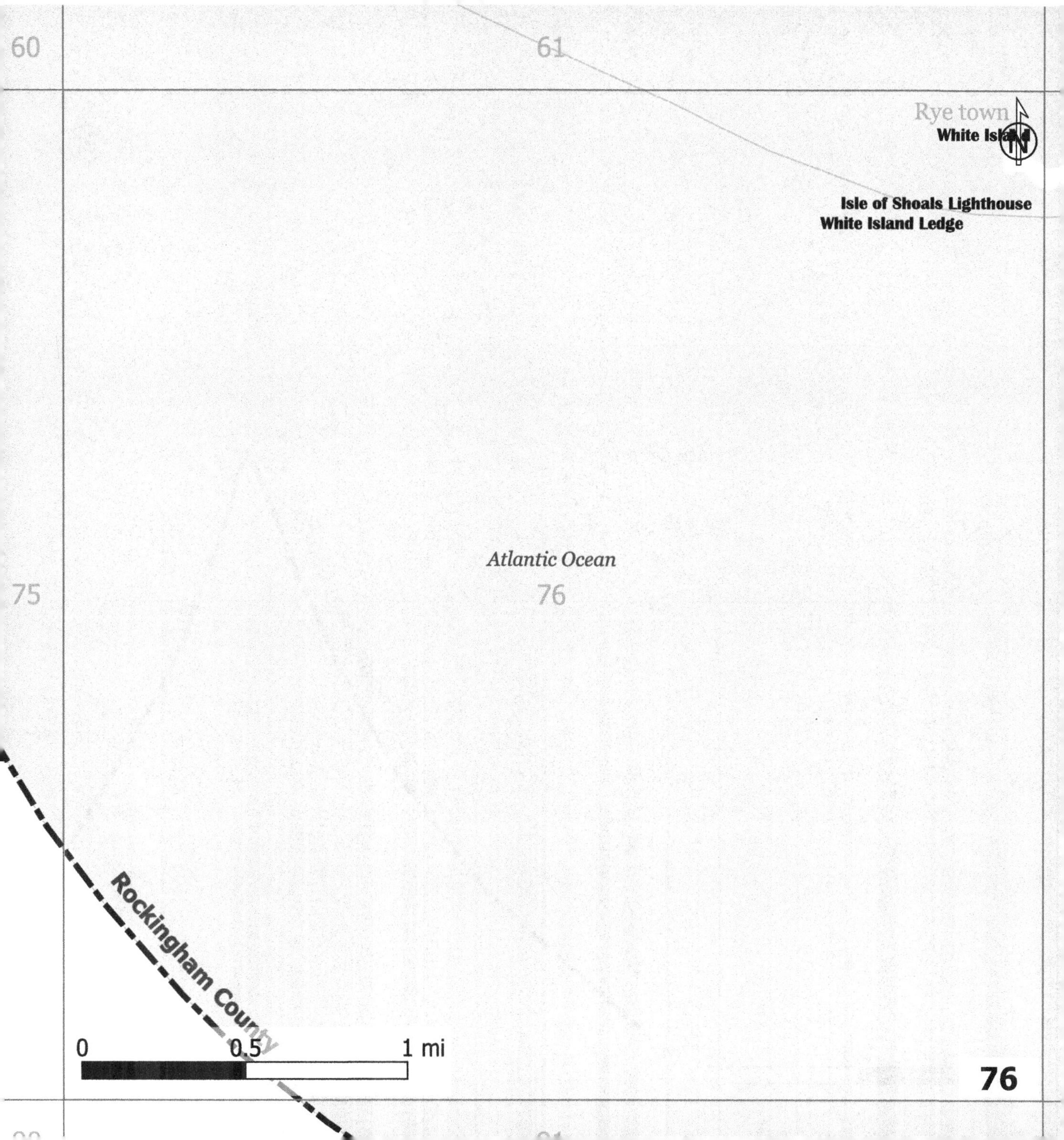

Rye town
White Island

Isle of Shoals Lighthouse
White Island Ledge

Atlantic Ocean

76

Rockingham County

0   0.5   1 mi

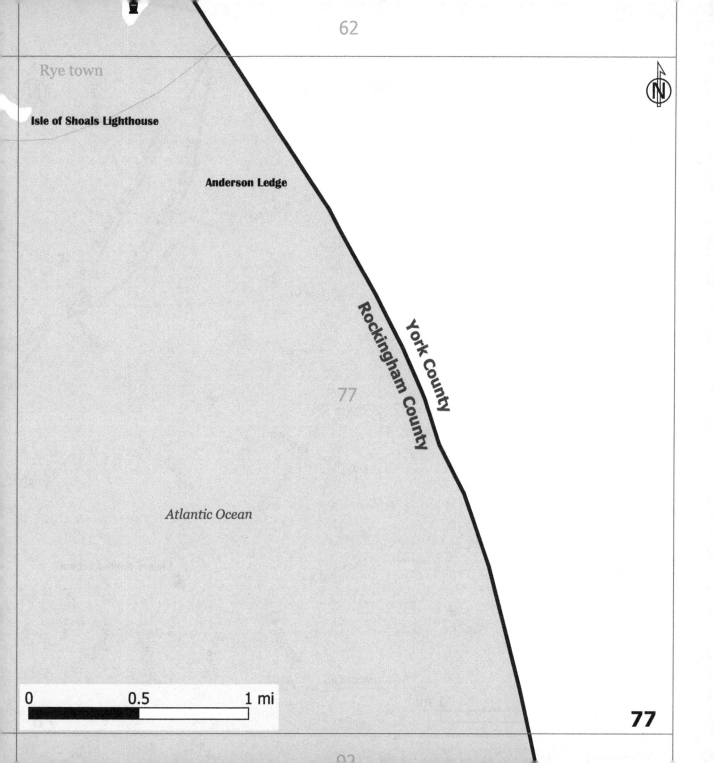

Rye town

Isle of Shoals Lighthouse

Anderson Ledge

Rockingham County

York County

77

Atlantic Ocean

N

| 0 | 0.5 | 1 mi |

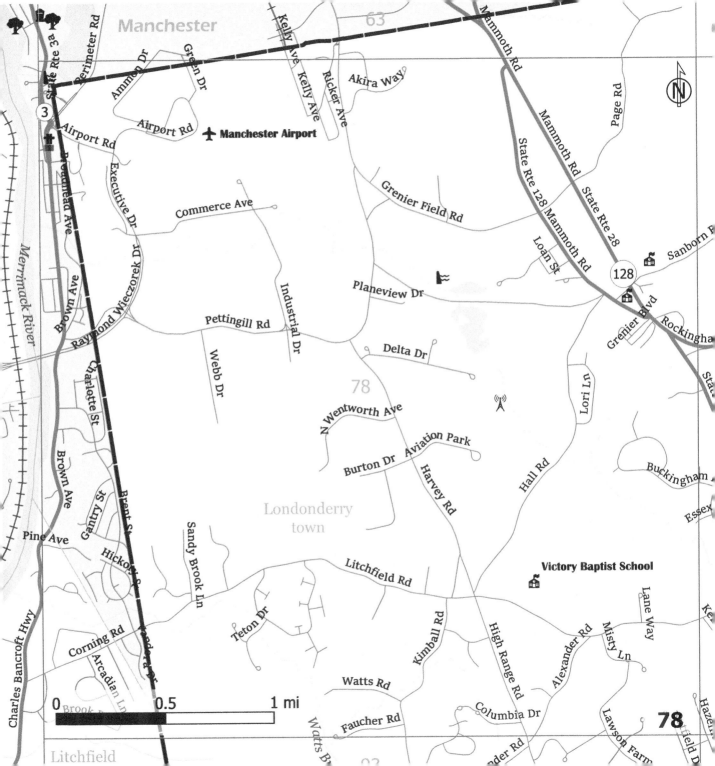

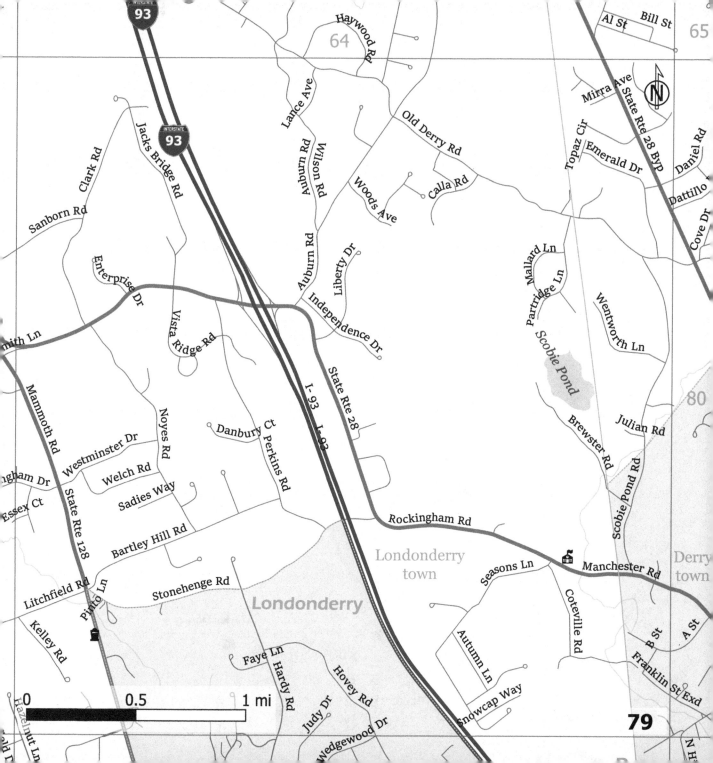

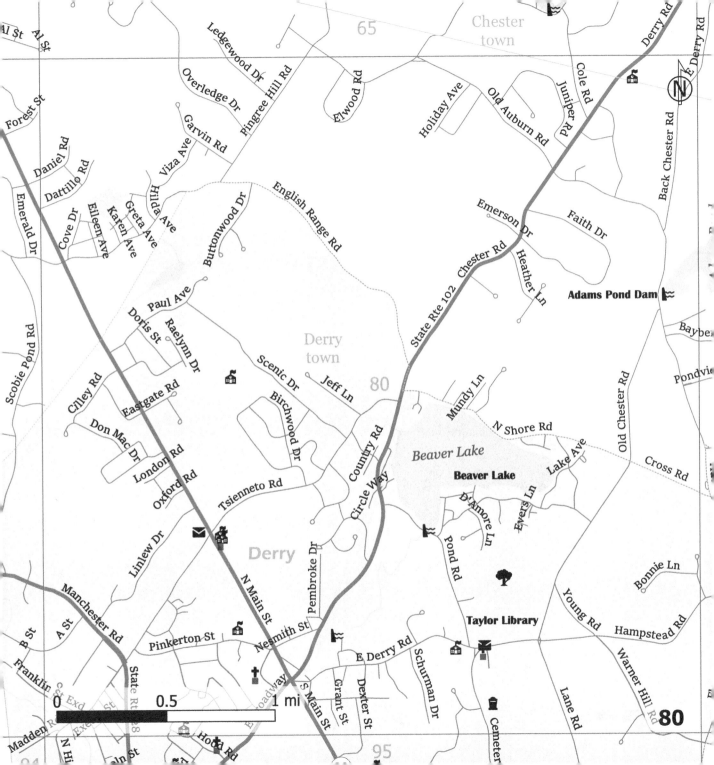

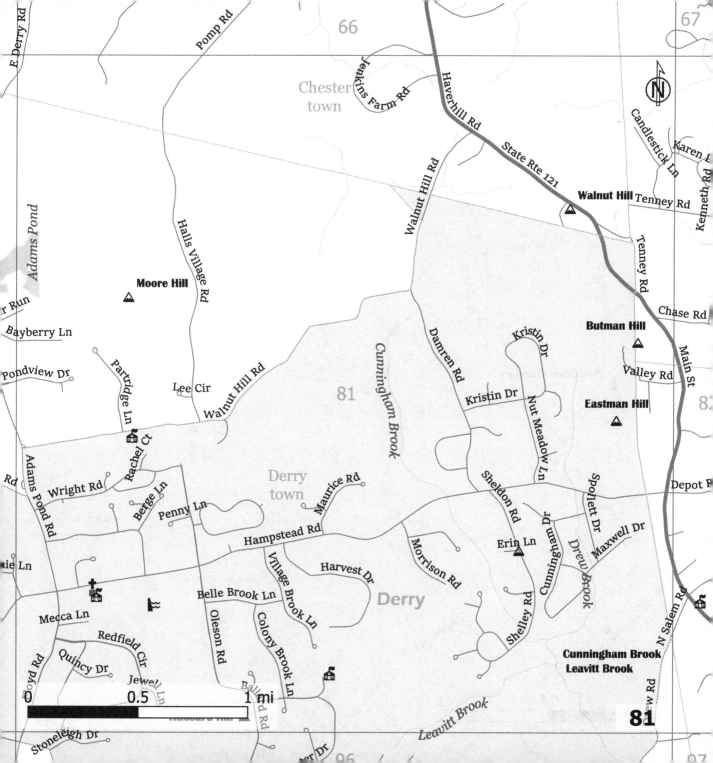

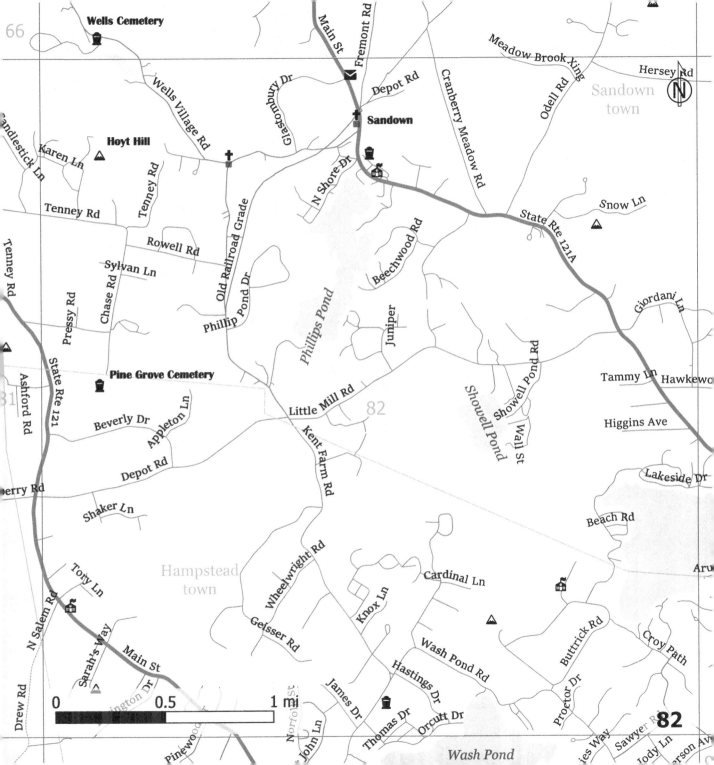

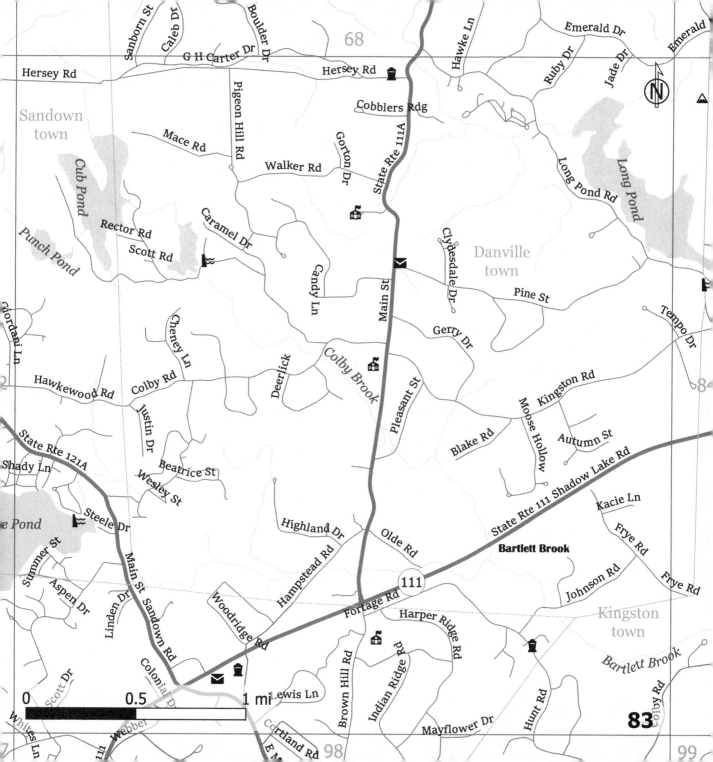

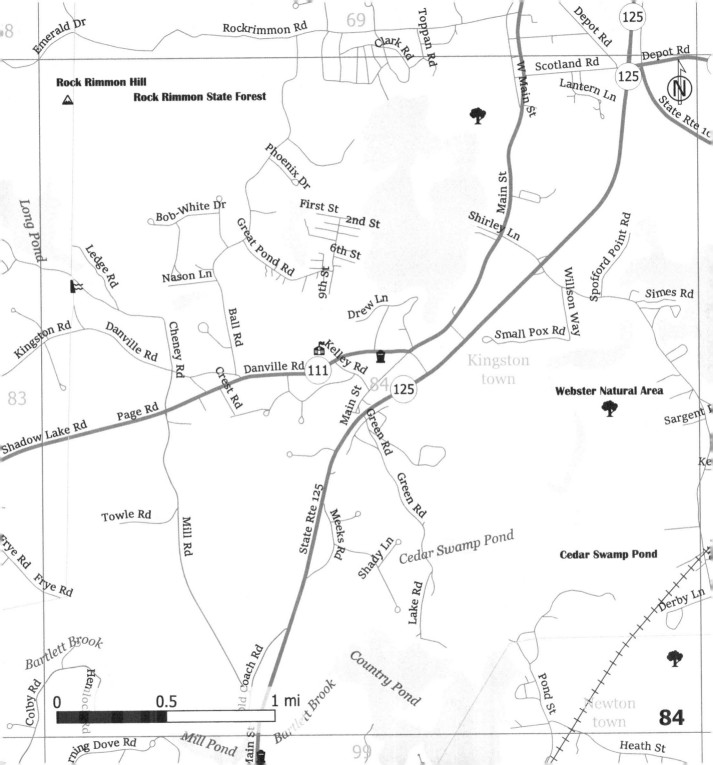

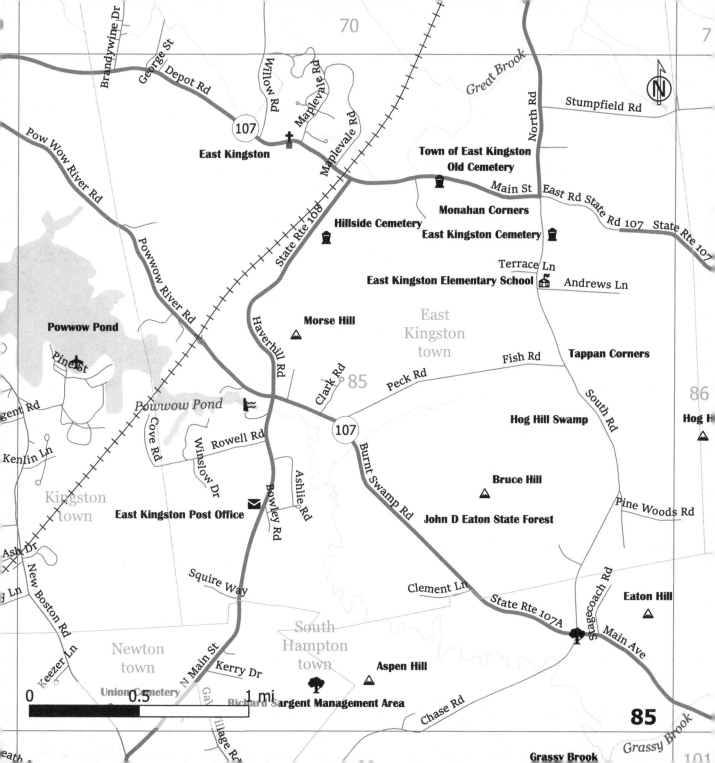

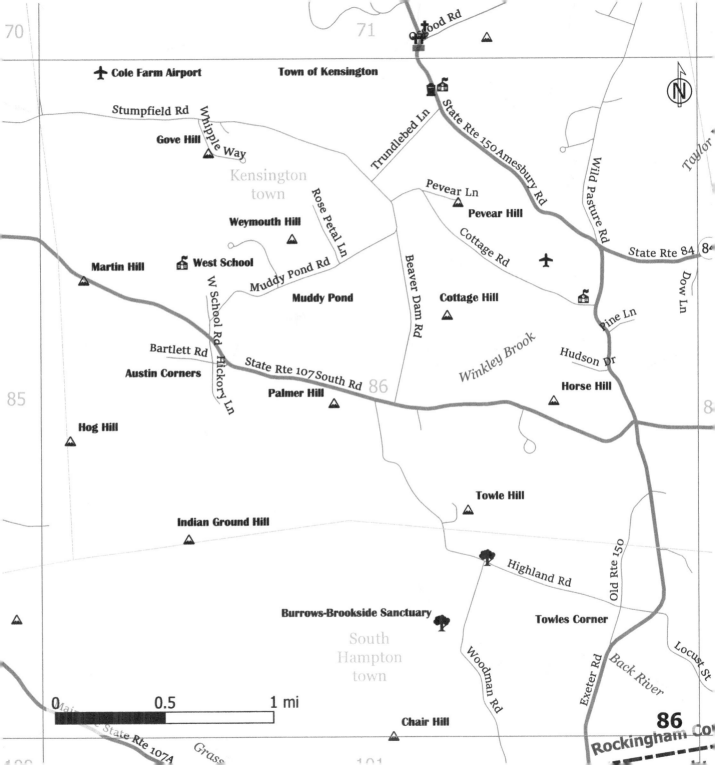

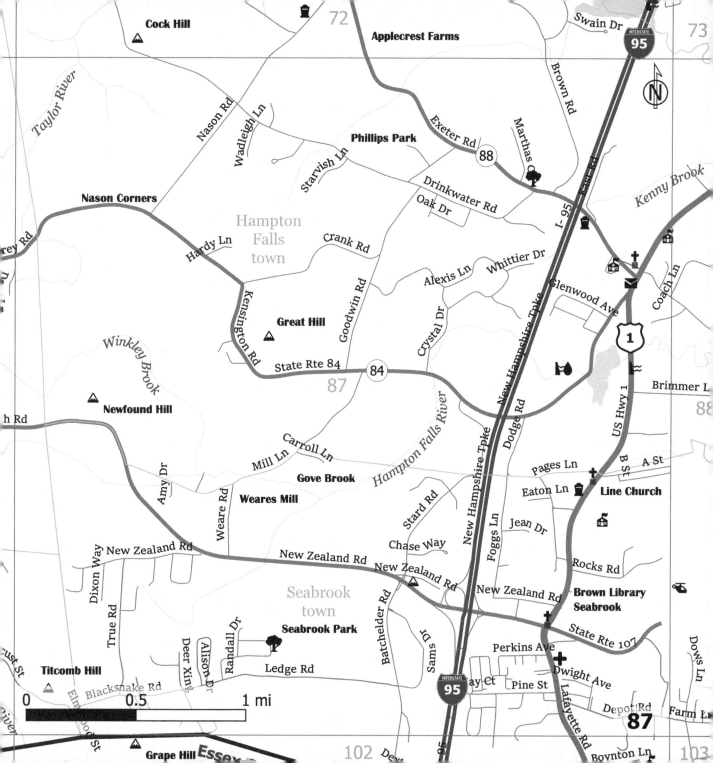

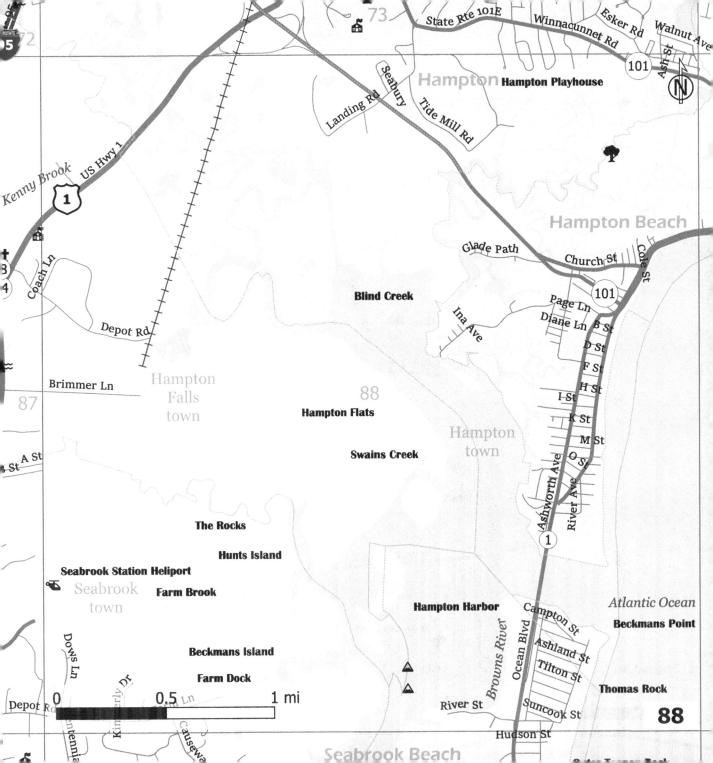

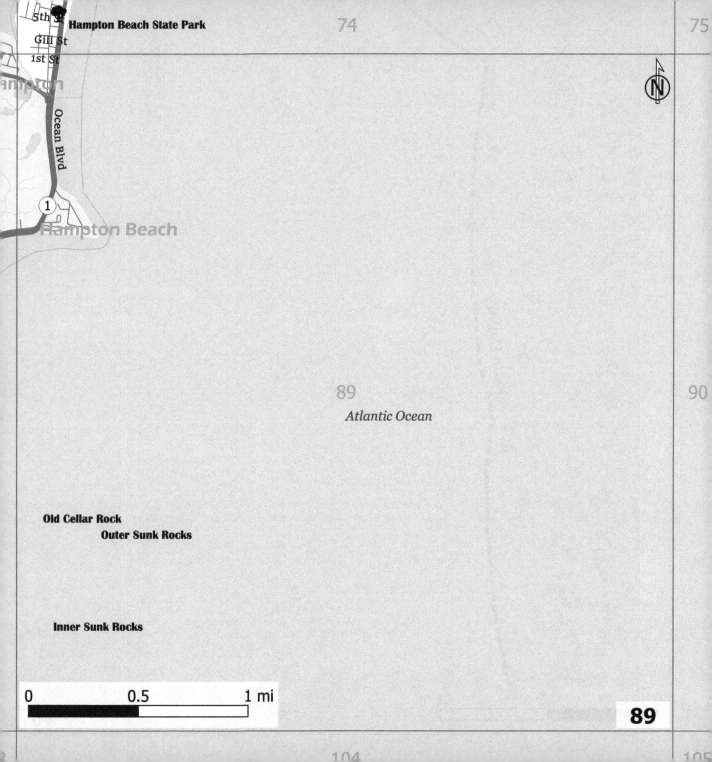

5th St
Hampton Beach State Park

Gill St

1st St

ampton

Ocean Blvd

(1)

Hampton Beach

Atlantic Ocean

Old Cellar Rock

Outer Sunk Rocks

Inner Sunk Rocks

0	0.5	1 mi

89

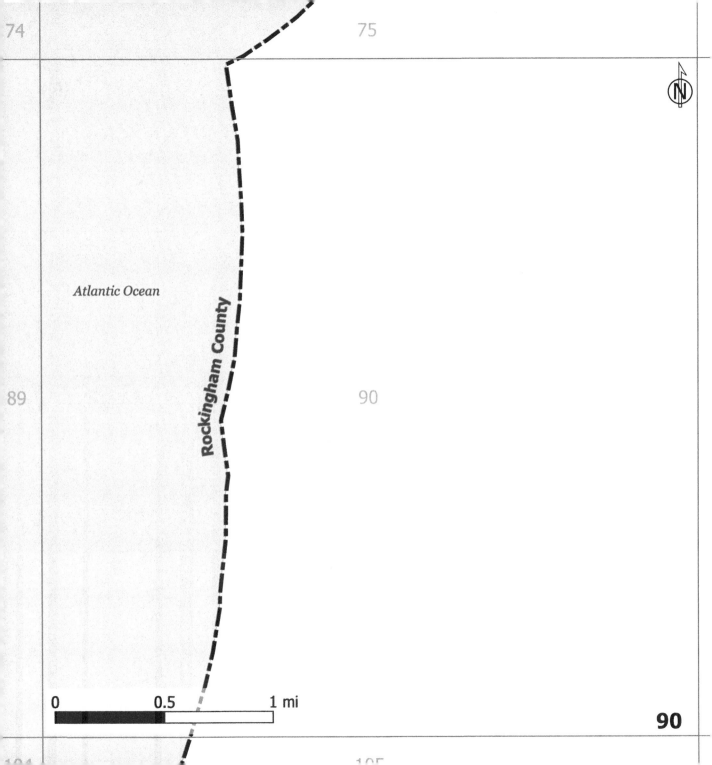

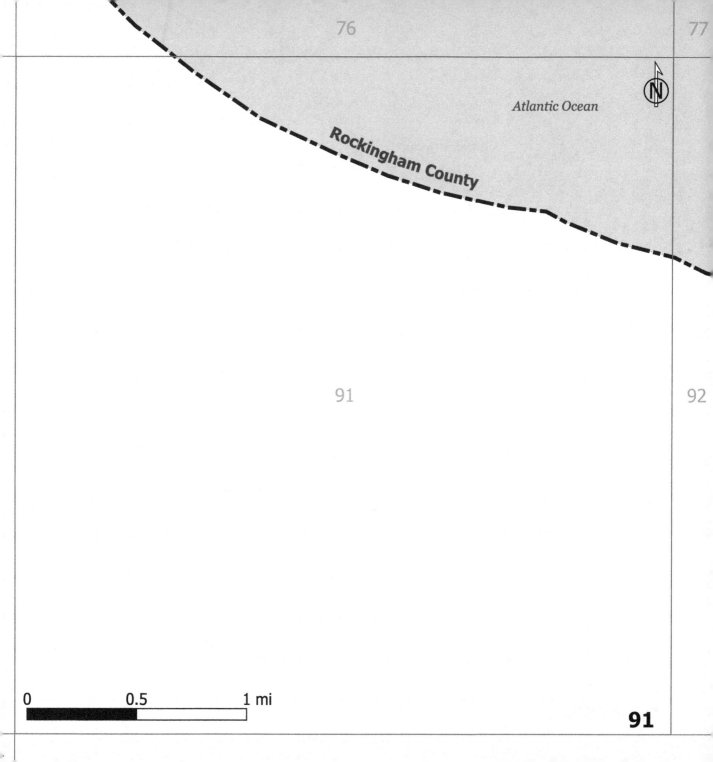

Atlantic Ocean

Rockingham County

0   0.5   1 mi

Atlantic Ocean

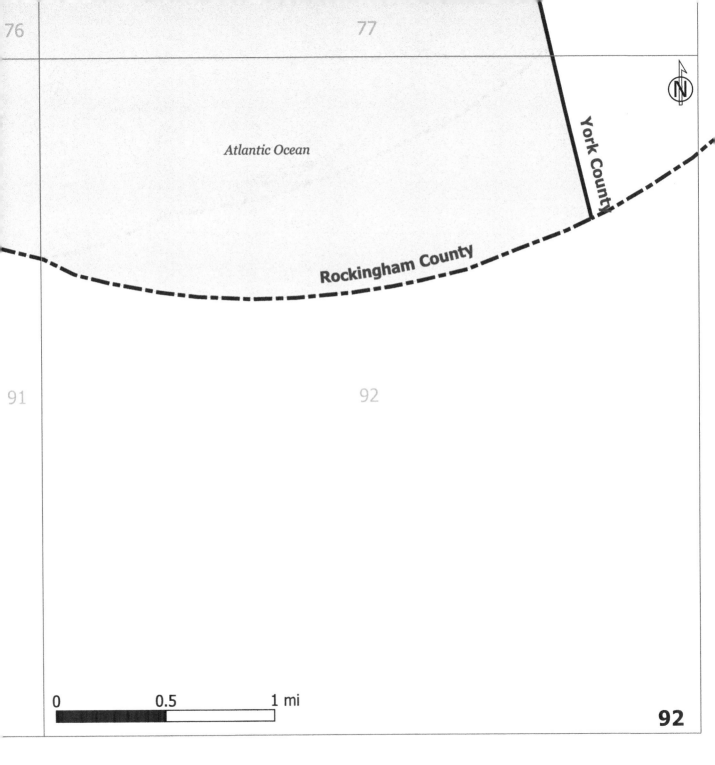

York County

Rockingham County

N

0   0.5   1 mi

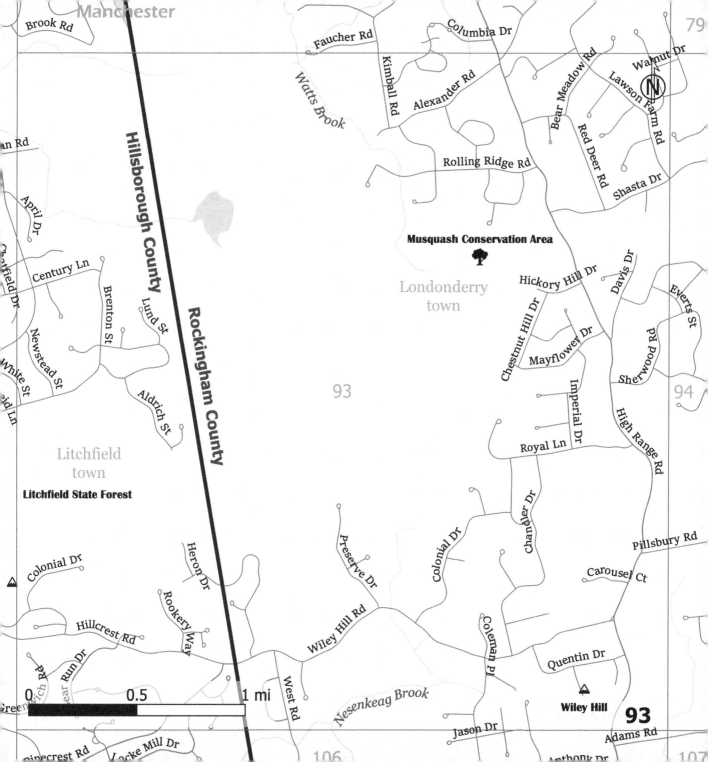

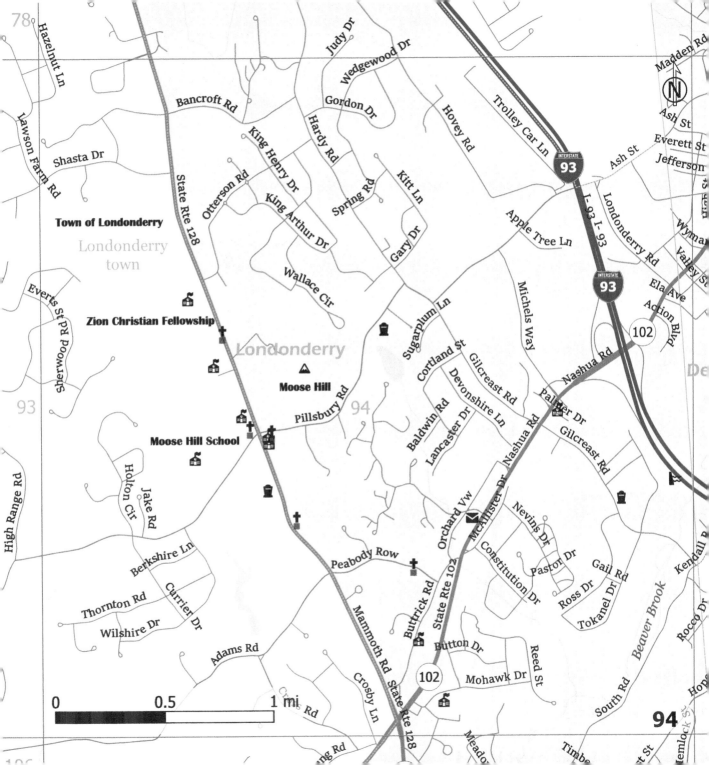

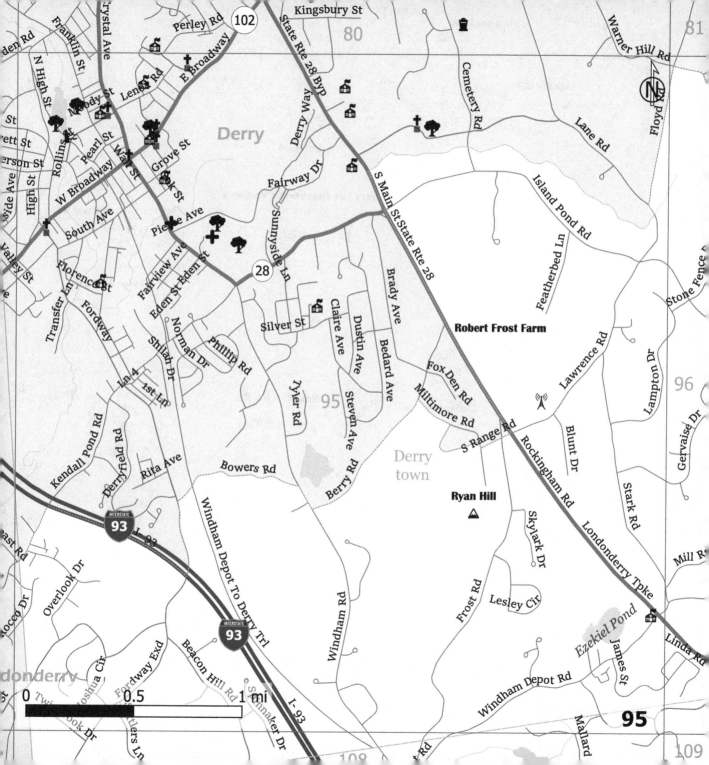

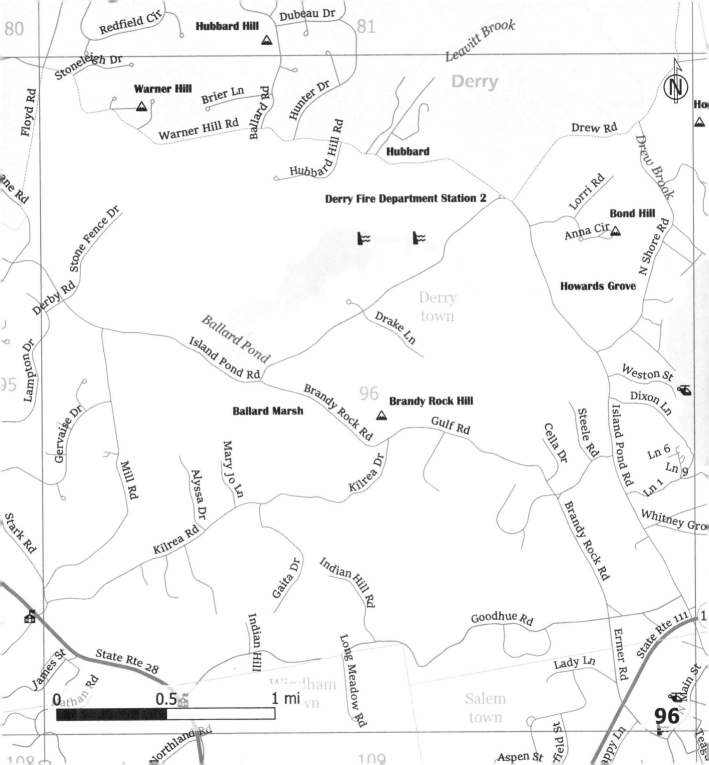

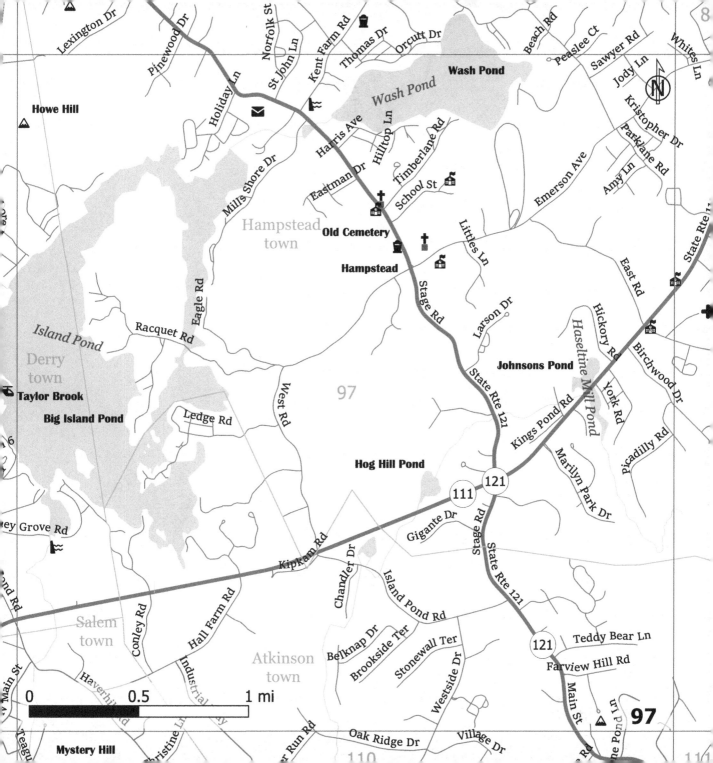

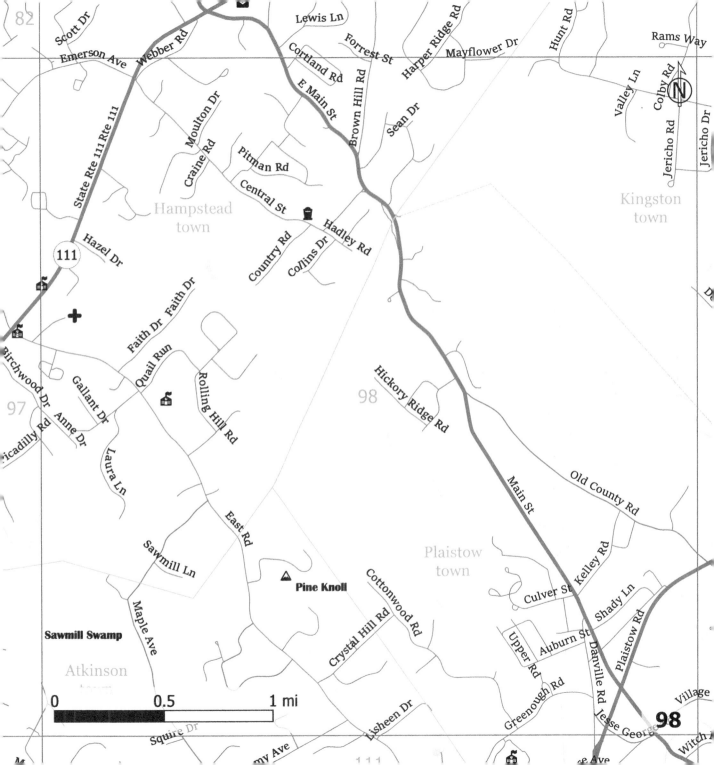

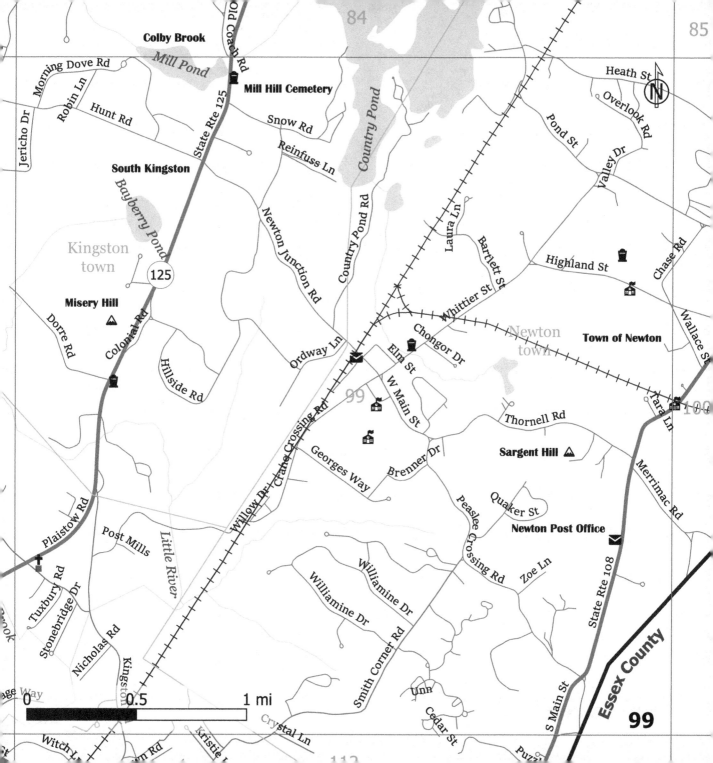

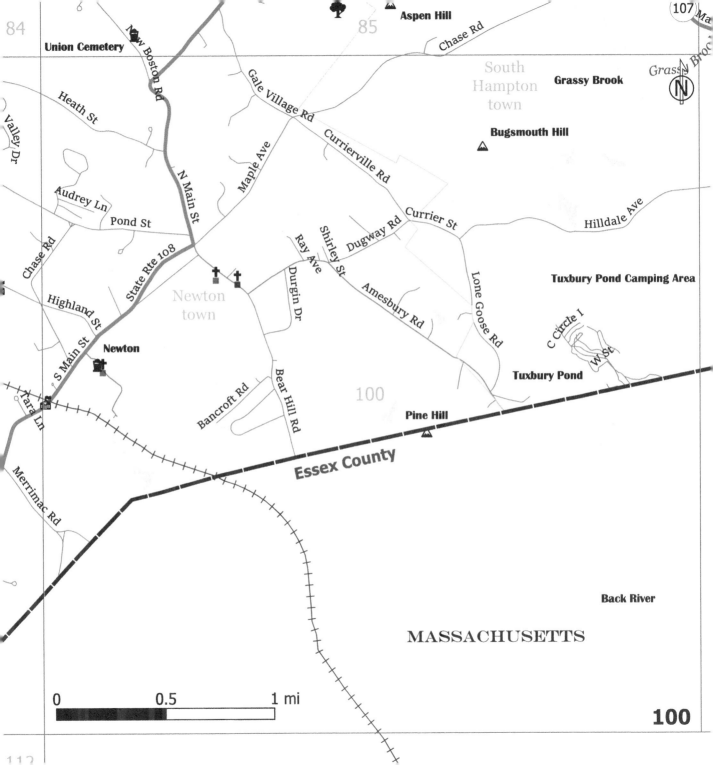

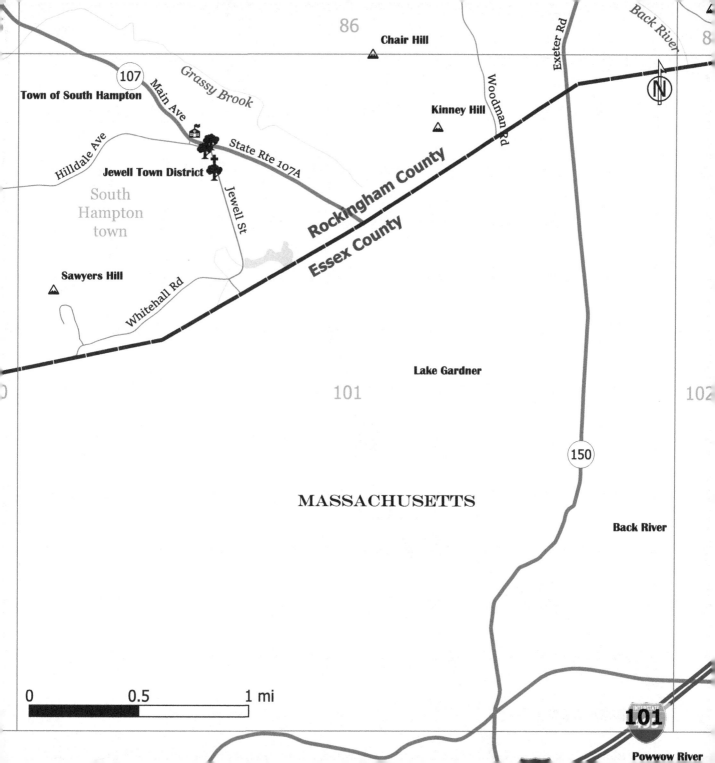

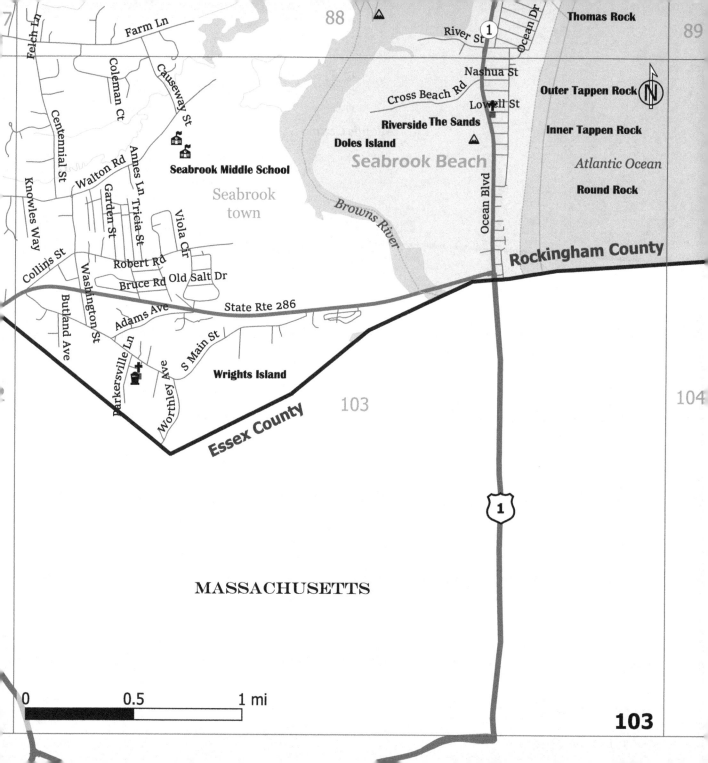

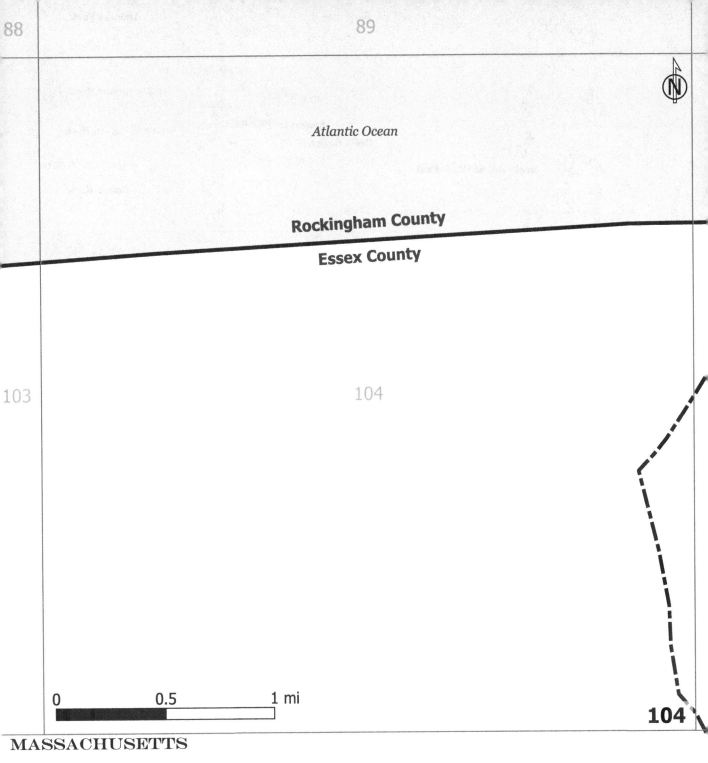

Atlantic Ocean

Rockingham County

Essex County

104

0   0.5   1 mi

104

MASSACHUSETTS

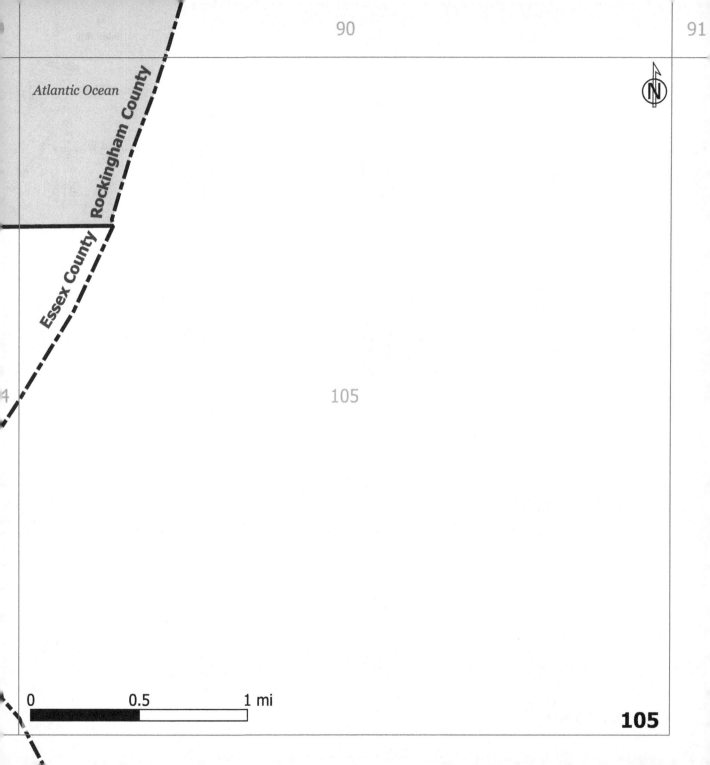

Atlantic Ocean

Rockingham County

Essex County

105

0   0.5   1 mi

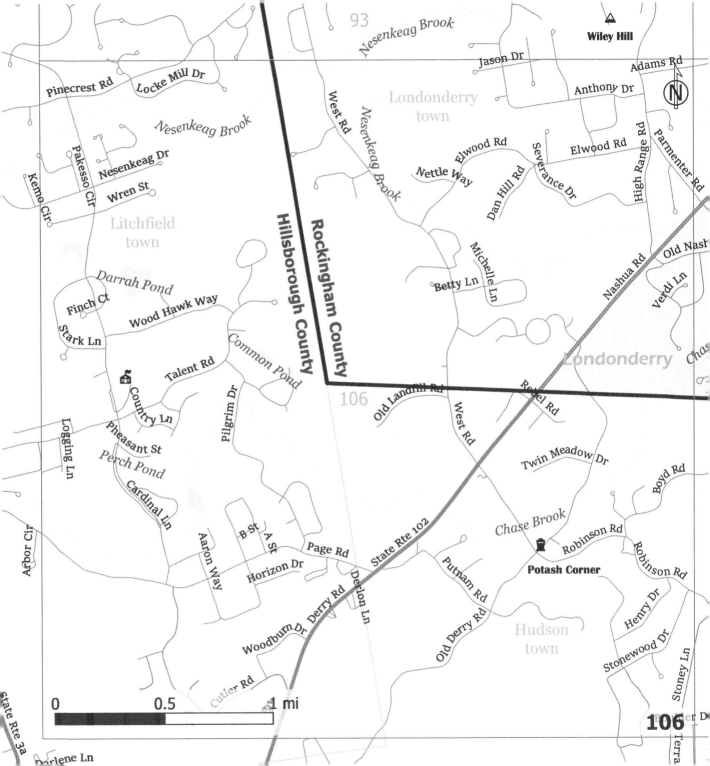

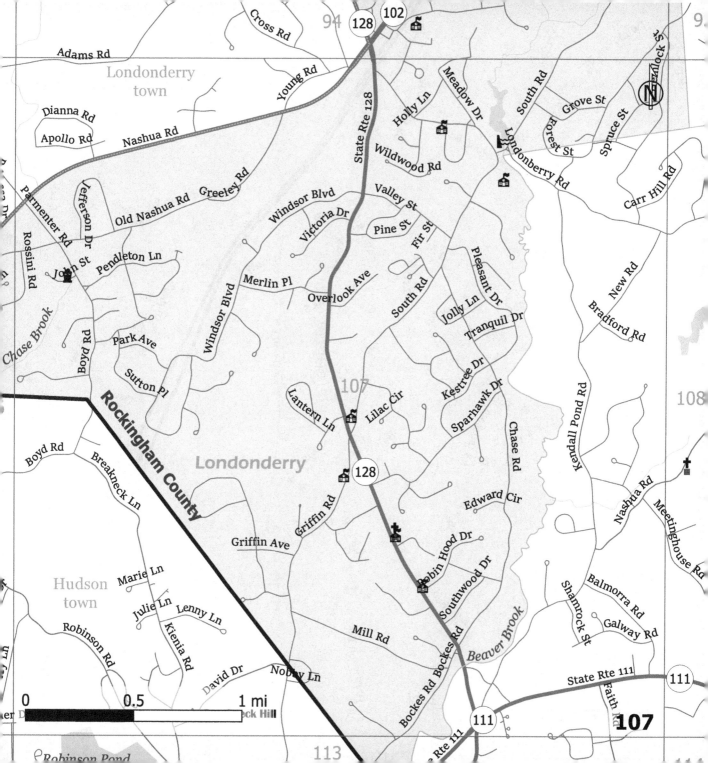

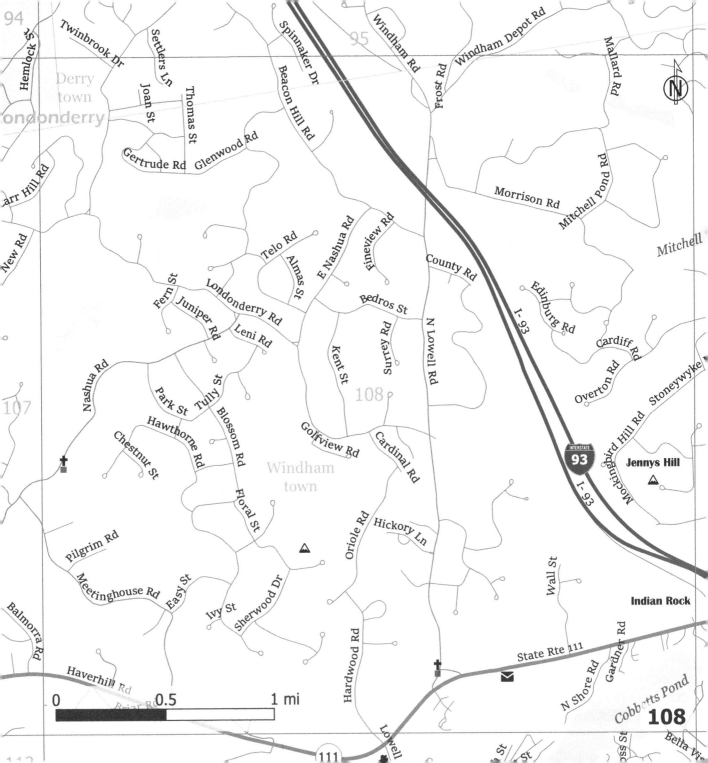

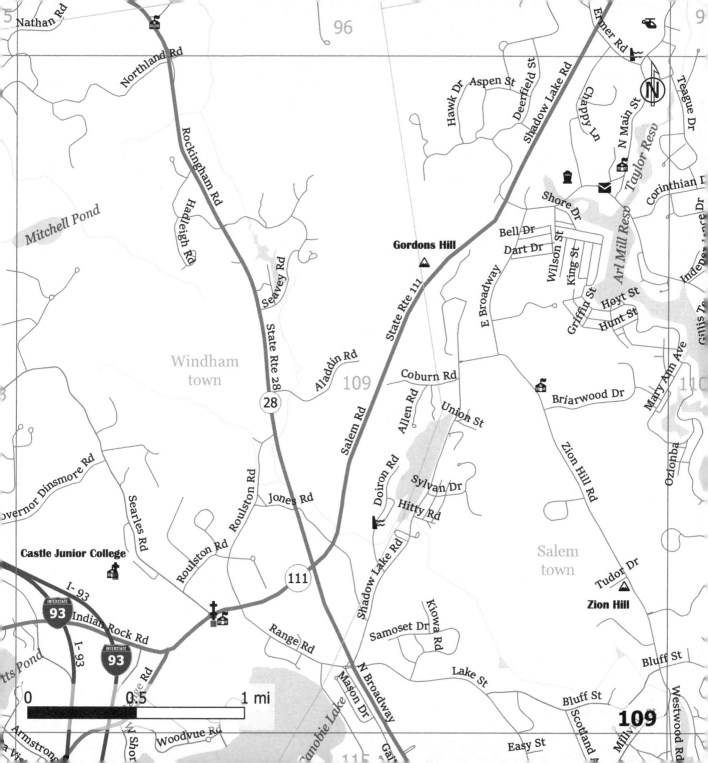

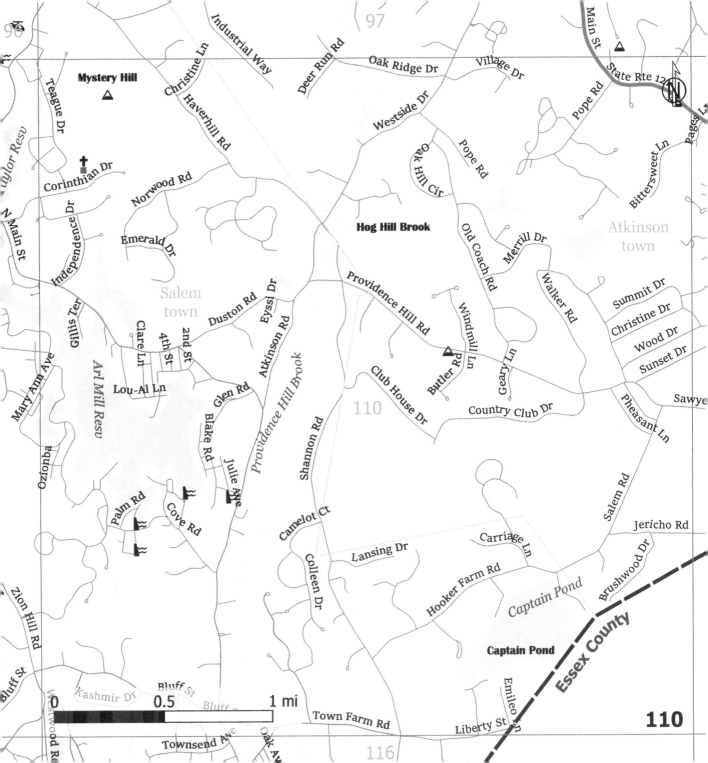

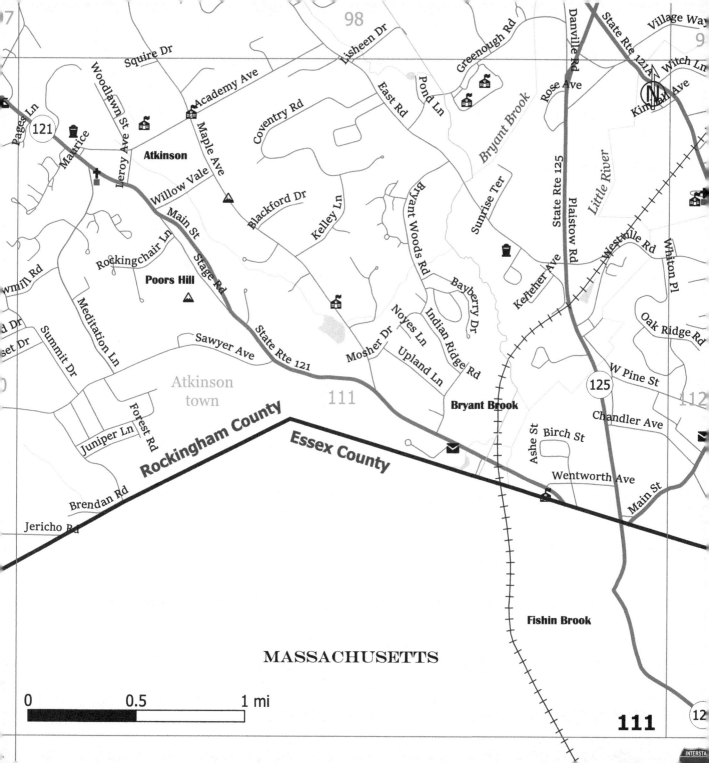

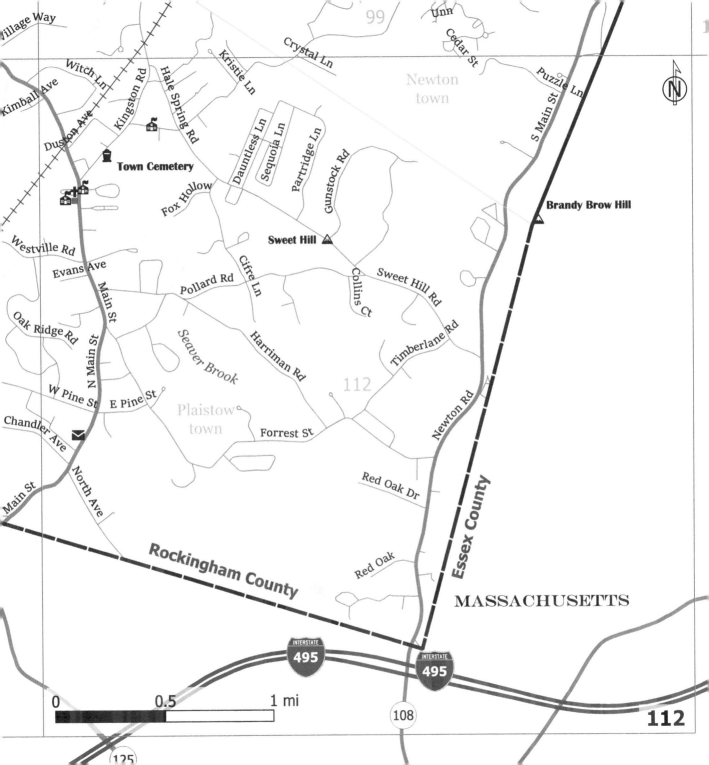

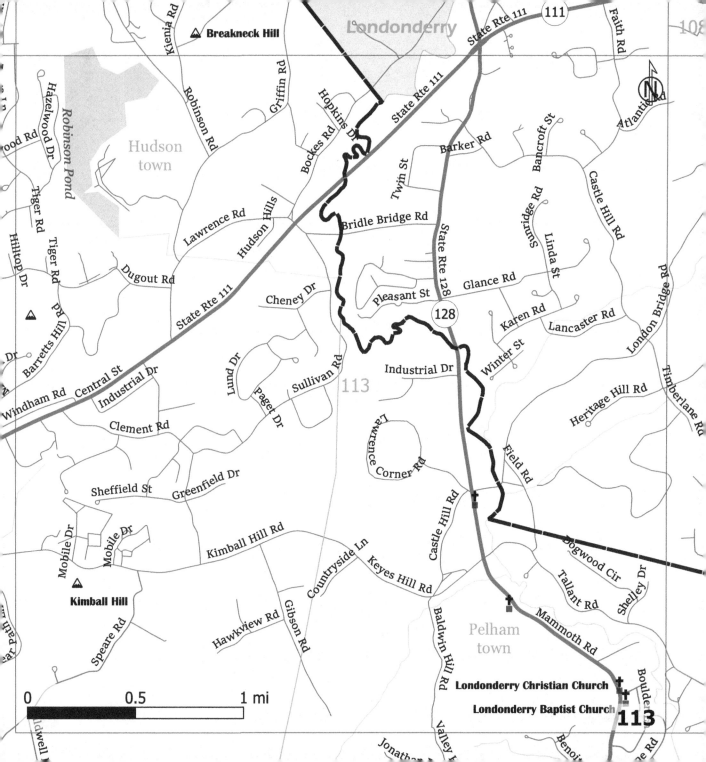

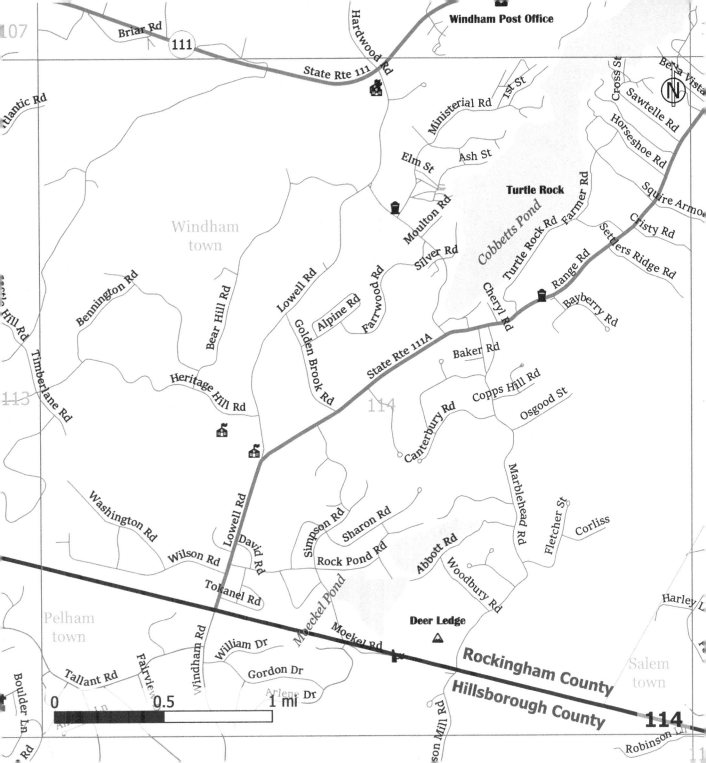

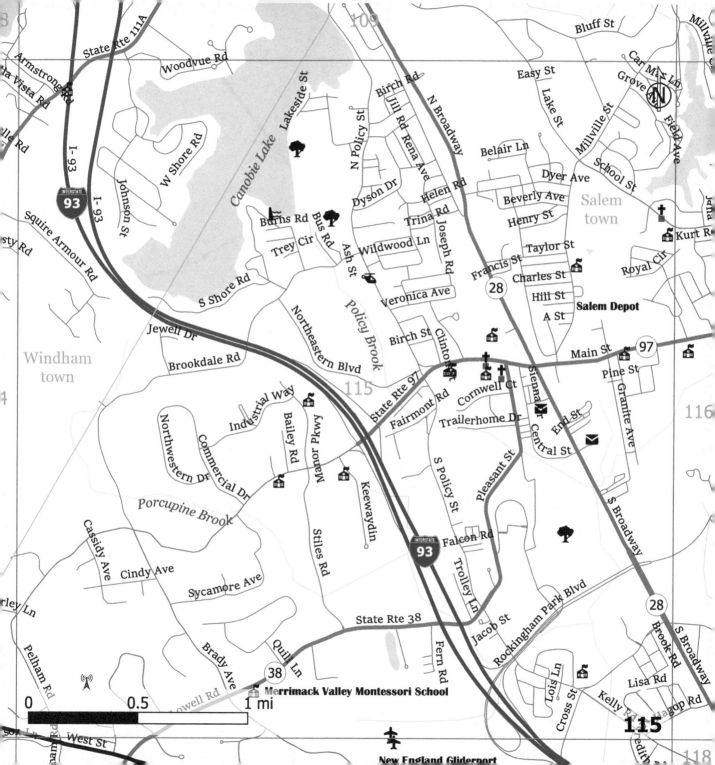

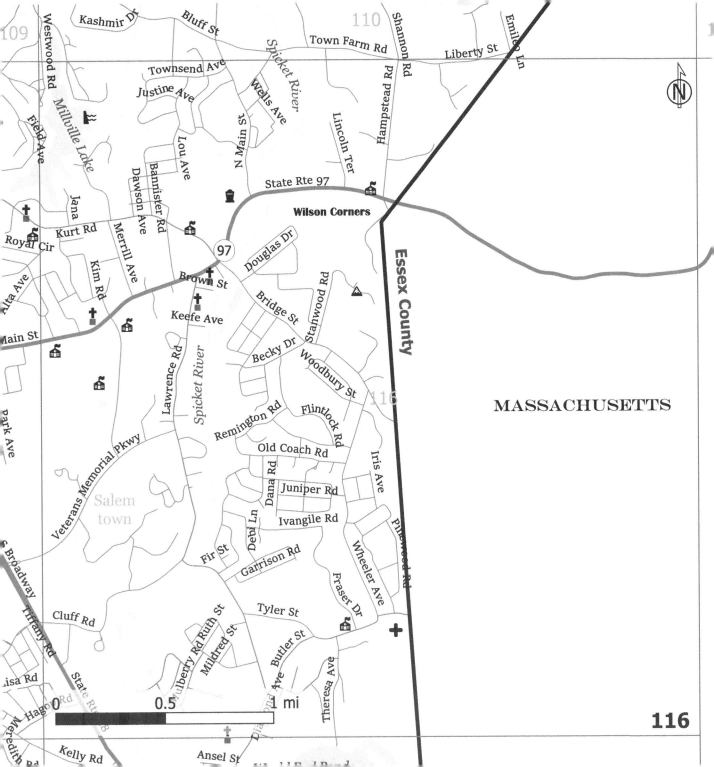

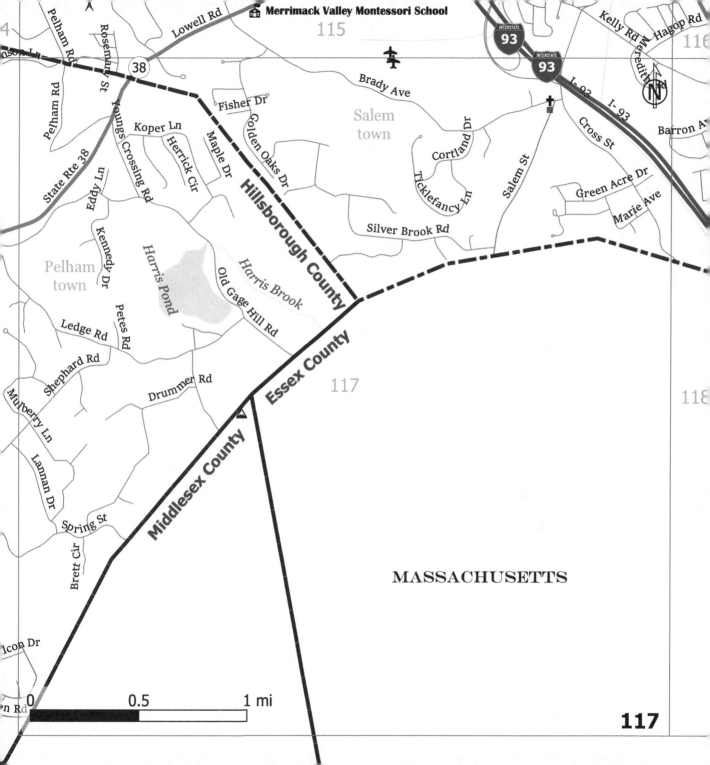

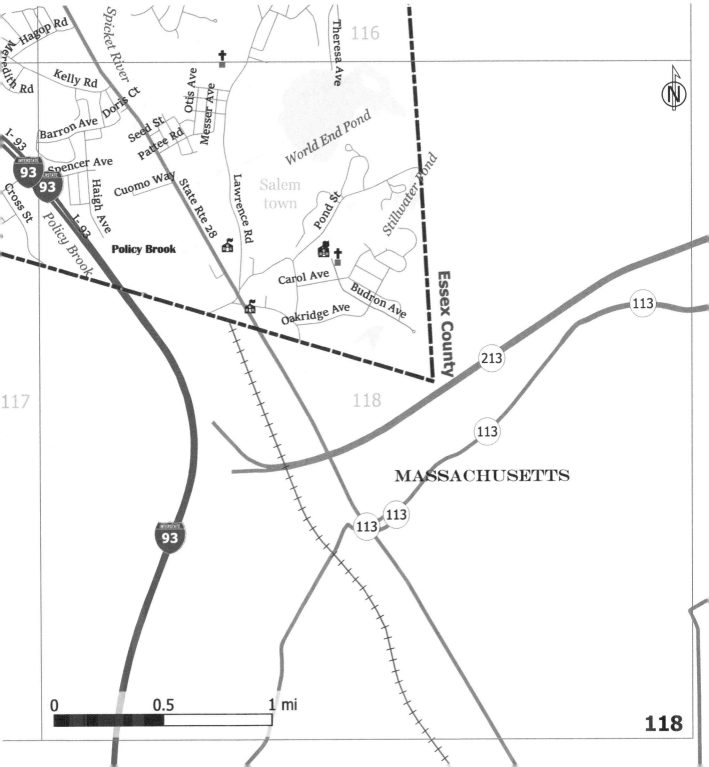

Made in the USA
Coppell, TX
06 September 2022

82721110R00070